Two Wheels North

Cycling the West Coast in 1909

by

Evelyn McDaniel Gibb

Oregon State University Press

Corvallis

The paper in this book meets the guidelines for permanence and durability of the Committee on Production Guidelines for Book Longevity of the Council on Library Resources and the minimum requirements of the American National Standard for Permanence of Paper for Printed Library Materials Z39.48-1984.

Library of Congress Cataloging-in-Publication Data
Gibb, Evelyn McDaniel.
  Two wheels North : cycling the West Coast in 1909 / by Evelyn McDaniel Gibb.— 1st ed.
    p. cm.
  ISBN 0-87071-485-6 (alk. paper)
  1. Pacific Coast (U.S.)—Description and travel. 2. Pacific States—Description and travel. 3. McDaniel, Victor, b. 1889—Journeys—Pacific Coast (U.S.) 4. Francisco, Ray, b. 1890?—Journeys—Pacific Coast (U.S.) 5. Cycling—Pacific Coast (U.S.) 6. Young men—California—Santa Rosa—Biography. 7. Santa Rosa (Calif.)—Biography. I. McDaniel, Victor, b. 1889. II. Francisco, Ray, b. 1890? III. Title.
  F852 .G45 2000
  917.904'31—dc21

                                        00-009771

Oregon State University Press
101 Waldo Hall
Corvallis OR 97331-6407
541-737-3166 • fax 541-737-3170
http://osu.orst.edu/dept/press

OREGON STATE
UNIVERSITY

This book is dedicated to

*Alexander and Tyler Lathum,
Victor McDaniel's great-grandsons,
who will break their own trails
of adventure in another new century.*

Acknowledgments

First to be recognized in a work such as this are family: my father, Victor McDaniel, for his story and his guidance in my relating of it; my mother, Ruth, who urged us on; my late husband, Gordon, for his belief in the project and in me; daughter Melissa Lathum and son Angus McKay, Jr., so enduringly supportive; and cousin Donna Carrillo Endicott, my reliable Santa Rosa consultant.

Thanks and gratitude are assuredly due the staffs of the many libraries and museums, large and small in northern California, Oregon and Washington who gave generously of their time to provide regional history and local data with which to enrich the narrative. I should particularly name Vonnie Matthews of *The Santa Rosa Press Democrat*'s News Research Center, whose help is much valued.

I am forever indebted to Martha Scharpf and Gloria Shagrun for their suggestions and unfailing willingness to read and reread the manuscript, to Nancy McKay for her good cheer while unsnarling my computer, to Steve Denzel, Peter Kahle, Natalie and Jack Lessinger, Jim Pravitz, Shelby Siems, and Nancy Wright, whose thoughtful critiques helped shape the book into readability.

My grateful thanks to the Oregon State University Press editors and staff for their confidence in this piece, and a special bow to Moira Dempsey, without whose talents the book would not be.

Foreword

❀ ❀ ❀

In the ninth year of the brash new twentieth century, the impossible was being either invented or conquered all the time. Travel by balloon would soon be commonplace. The Wright Brothers were sure folks would someday fly about in aeroplanes, though theirs had plowed the ground again in March when the propeller caught a rudder rope. In April Robert Peary drove his dog sled four hundred miles so he could stand on the North Pole. Talk was that a Ford automobile had won a race from the east coast to the west. And already, two electric automobiles tooled quietly about the streets of Santa Rosa. The decade was one of exuberance and daring.

Two Wheels North is the story of a fifty-four-day bicycle trip made in 1909 by two young men just out of high school, Victor McDaniel and Ray Francisco. Bound for the Alaska-Yukon-Pacific Exposition in Seattle, Washington, they set off from their home in Santa Rosa, California, on second-hand Acme and Cleveland bicycles to pedal, push, and walk the nearly thousand miles. Travel was over roads of dust and ruts, over corduroy made of logs and even corn stalks, along paths beside the railroad, or (where the path disappeared) over the ties. If they found no road or railroad, they trudged cross-country, whatever the terrain.

A few Santa Rosans had journeyed the distance by steamer and by train, but none had completed the trip north by team, automobile or stage. Vic and Ray's bicycles had always taken them where they wanted to go; they would be the first from town to travel to Seattle overland not by rail.

Such a bold venture intrigued Santa Rosa's newspaper editor, Ernest Finley. He suggested the young men write letters about their adventures and mail them to him along the way. For this he would ask the *Seattle Post Intelligencer* to pay them a munificent twenty-five dollars (almost as much as Vic's father earned as a carpet layer in a whole month) when, or rather if, the young men reached the fair. And so it was that on a warm August morning Vic and Ray, ripe with vigor and the image of themselves as town heroes, pedaled loaded bicycles out Fourth Street to become ambassadors of the *Santa Rosa Press Democrat*.

In his later years my father, Victor McDaniel, lived next door to me, giving us many opportunities to talk. Around my parents' small kitchen table I asked him questions I hadn't the interest or intellect to ask as a young person—about his childhood, his parents, his three sisters, high school basketball, track. I soon learned he valued one of his life's experiences more than any other: "When Ray and I rode our bicycles all the way from Santa Rosa up to Seattle's Alaska-Yukon-Pacific-Exposition." In his words I heard the vigor of youth. His failing eyes sparked. His rounded shoulders squared. For the next few years Dad and I looked forward to the hour, sometimes two, we spent talking every day, usually about "the best friend I ever had," and "the trip that made me a man." Together we read the densely written picture post cards he sent home, and the long, detailed letters published in the *Santa Rosa Press Democrat*. It was during these sharings and the memories they stirred in my father that I became alert to the occasional phrase that brought him erect, the recollections of encounters or snippets of banter that turned his old eyes boyish.

So I began note-taking. Each morning I read Dad my typed notes from the day before. He would then emend, add on, scratch out: "That's not just how it was," or "I forgot to mention. . . ." When I asked why he hadn't bothered to recount these incidents in his letters or post cards, he explained, "Heroes in those days, well, it wouldn't do to admit fear or uncertainty or a lot of other things, not for folks back home to read about."

Two Wheels North attempts to convey some of the exuberance and passion I heard and saw in him as he relived those experiences. With dialog drawing on my memory of his speech patterns and penchant for word pictures, I let him tell his story. In words I think Dad would have used, he shares his excitements and fears. Often in contrast, the quotes in the chapter leads allow the reader to view the trip as portrayed by the would-be heroes to their admirers back home.

So come along for the ride.

A note to the reader

Details of the postcards reproduced in the text can be found at the back of the book, starting on page 181.

Where no credit is given for a photograph, the photographer is unknown.

Excerpts from the *Santa Rosa Press Democrat* are used with permission.

1

People are making all sorts of efforts to get to the Seattle
Exposition, but it has remained for Victor McDaniel and Ray
Francisco, two well-known young men of this city, to make the
trip by wheel. They will go as representatives of the *Press
Democrat*, and propose to make the journey by wheel both
ways if such a thing is possible. One of the principal objects of
the trip is to ascertain just what difficulties are encountered in
a long bicycle trip overland, and report the same for the
readers of this paper.

The start will be made on or about August 9 and the nervy
travelers are already getting their equipment (and
themselves) in condition. They propose to carry their baggage
with them, on frames of special construction built on the front
and rear of their wheels.

THE *SANTA ROSA PRESS DEMOCRAT*

Between May and August Ray and I argued with our folks, but
we'd made up our minds. They said we should think about
things awhile longer. Barely through high school, we weren't
old enough to set out on a wild and dangerous journey. Our
mothers cried, but mostly off by themselves. After all, we told them,
Ray and I were not only grown, we now had a responsibility to our
sponsor, Mr. Finley, the editor of the newspaper. We promised to
write him letters every few days telling of our experiences. In return,
at the Alaska-Yukon-Pacific Exposition we would receive twenty-five
dollars from the *Seattle Post Intelligencer*. We told our folks we
would try to save the money and come back on our bicycles. But
they knew, as we did, after riding the thousand or so miles up there
we'd likely use the money for passage home on the steamer or train.

On the morning of August 9, 1909, our official picture was taken
in front of the *Santa Rosa Press Democrat*. They had to take a
second one because somebody forgot to close the doors for the first
one. Besides, the little Connelly boy edged himself in. People

Victor McDaniel (right) and Ray Francisco on the morning of August 9, 1909, are studied by a young admirer. Photograph courtesy of *Santa Rosa Press Democrat*

standing around to see us off let Mama and Mrs. Francisco through so they could give us one last wet-cheeked goodbye. As we set off, bald Mr. Jenkins from the bike shop called out, "Safe wheeling to the fair, boys!"

We pedaled up Mendocino Avenue and waved behind us till the crowd broke up. My eyes filmed over because I knew Mama was crying. I was careful not to look at Ray alongside, but I could tell he sat grim and out of rhythm with his Cleveland. After the turn to Fourth Street, I stood on the pedals to power the wheels through the oiled dirt and blinked my eyes several times to clear them. My forty-pound load felt balanced; I was of a piece with my Sears Roebuck Acme King.

"Only some better than two months now before that fair closes," Ray hollered over. "You really think we can make it? In time?"

In front of us the sprinkling wagon dribbled its jagged trail of dust puffs from the cans in back. Ray passed on the left. I moved right so I could take one last look at the colossal Indian Frank Muther just installed in front of his cigar store. Once ahead of the team, side by side we crossed D Street.

"People say the roads are wetted down through the valley, some places even oiled," I said. "Beyond the valley it's a blank slate. But there's stage roads over the mountains. Our rail maps'll get us through. In time too."

I stood on the pedals again so he wouldn't see my face. Ray had a way of knowing when I was unsure, when I was down deep afraid.

From the day we saw the Alaska-Yukon-Pacific Exposition traveling tent show I'd talked hard to convince Ray we could bike the thousand miles up there to see the fair. I had to go, and Ray had to go with me. He was my best friend. In spite of his wanting to study to be a preacher, he was my best friend. We did everything together. But Mallory Brothers Blacksmithing had taken longer to make the racks than we planned. Then there was the two months of work in the orchards to earn money for the racks, and the Dunlops, and the canvas for the baggage pouches Ray's mother made. Our travel time had been dangerously narrowed. And now, after buying a new Iver-Johnson revolver, a used Pieper .22 boy's rifle, a cyclometer, and a hatchet, the five dollars and sixty-five cents I carried was all the money we had.

Crossing MacDonald Avenue I looked down to where the Civil War's Grand Army of the Republic encampment turned Veterans Park into a mammoth bivouac every Flag Day week. Would I ever again see that town of big white tents? Or hear those fellows tell their stories and sing their songs around the campfires? The bike's steady rhythm leaned me, side to side, maybe this day's only certainty.

"You bring that billiken?" I yelled over, like it didn't matter one way or the other.

"In my blanket roll," Ray hollered and swerved around a flapping banty hen.

It was at the fair's traveling tent show in May, after we'd seen the real Siberian Eskimos and listened to the high-hatted spieler tell about the Igorot people from the Philippines who would cook and eat their puppies where folks could watch, and the Hawaiian girl, Ieka, who would dance her native hula-hula at the Pay Streak Carnival, that the fellow held up a little clay figure. "Twenty-five cents buys you this imp of a billiken," he'd chanted. "Get a patron spirit of the fair. 'God of Things That Ought to Be.' Only twenty-five cents buys you every good luck." Ray had jammed a hand down his trouser pocket

Billiken, God of Things that Ought to Be, the patron spirit of the Alaska-Yukon-Pacific Exposition. Photograph: Seattle Museum of History and Industry

and brought up a two-bit piece. Neither of us believed the story about the good luck, of course, but ever since that night we took care to bring the silly three-inch-tall piece with us wherever we went. The billiken might not be able to put us on the right road, but carrying him was a queer sort of comfort.

Just out of town, opposite the board sign with the dim letters, "Keep to the middle of the road to Keegan Brothers," Ray dropped back. Neither of us had ever bought clothes from Keegan Brothers, but the sign was important: this was where the sprinkling wagon turned around. From here on, the road was dust and ruts. I bounced along at the same pace, increasing the distance between us, my wheels churning up brown clouds.

Back there Ray's doubts would fester. I knew my friend. He wasn't really afraid of the trip, just worried we couldn't do it. Or that we wouldn't live up to the promises we'd made to Mr. Finley and other folks in Santa Rosa. October 1, the date the Seattle paper was to pay us our twenty-five dollars, was less than eight weeks off. And for at least two, maybe three of those weeks we'd have to work along the way to make the money we needed to get there. Ray's worries were solid. It just wouldn't do for me to agree with him. That is, not so he'd know.

A black, woolly dog ran barking out of an acacia-lined drive at the old Duggan place and chased after me. Sighting Ray, he bounded off to bite at his wheels. Yes, with the worry in Ray I'd be smart not to tell him the tales I'd picked up at the free lunch tables in the saloons, about the animals that roamed the mountains, and the rapscallions who prowled that bandit country up in the Siskiyous. At the time I'd resented his not going with me to the Fourth Street drinking houses to eat. Now I was glad.

On the long coast down Mileta Hill, he hollered up, "Want to stop by the stone quarry?"

"Sure. Lighten our load. Eat that chicken Mama fried up."

We leaned the bikes against the trunk of a live oak laced with Spanish moss and flopped on the bleached grass by the creek, just as we'd done on many an afternoon. I slipped the pack from my back, unbuckled the strap and pulled out the wrapping-paper package. This day was the same, yet different. On a usual Monday the Italian workmen across the creek would call to one another in their tongue, their hammers striking chisels and pounding out the devil's own tattoo as they sculpted chunks of stone into paving blocks for San Francisco's streets that had been chewed up and spit out by the big quake. But now the quarry was silent, not even a voice to be heard.

"No work today," I said, a chicken leg in each hand.

"Some kind of Italian holiday. You want to write the first article to Finley?"

"Doesn't matter. We'll both sign though. The one writes the article can sign his name first, how's that?"

"Sounds fair." We laughed at the pun.

Up over the rock face a hawk wheeled, banked and looped low to settle atop a hill pine. I couldn't remember I'd ever seen a hawk quite there before. The day's wind must be just right, or the quiet from the quarry an unusual quality for him too. But inside myself I knew the difference was more, much more.

2

A large crowd gathered Monday morning at the *Press Democrat* office to witness the departure of Victor McDaniel and Ray Francisco on their bicycle trip to the Seattle Exposition. The boys were clad in bicycle pants and sweaters but carried extra clothing. . . . They are confident that the trip will prove very enjoyable as well as instructive. . . . From here the proposed route lies via Sonoma, Napa, Vacaville, Winters."

THE *SANTA ROSA PRESS DEMOCRAT*

Thick dust, fine as talc, overlaid the dirt road to the Valley of the Moon. Trees—toyons, oaks, and madrones—masked in dust, marched on either side like soldiers in the same army.

"That'll be some fine house Jack London's gonna build up there," I hollered over my shoulder, nodding to the right where oaks greened the rolling hills, then sat back in the saddle and prepared to coast down. Jack London had just returned from his trip to South America, or so the paper reported, saying he was eager to start the construction of a fine lodge.

Outside of Sonoma we pedaled up a gentle grade and, for the first time, entered unfamiliar country. The dirt road was winding and with few passing pullouts. Stand on the pedals, weight forward, grunt down, ease up, side to side, right, left. The grade sharpened and pain shot through my thighs. Here I was a track man, and already tired. Ray's legs would be screaming. At the top, puffing, I planted my feet to either side, leaned myself slack in the saddle and pushed back my cap. There he was, in an envelope of dust, pulling around the lower turn. Ray was a sure-enough friend. He wouldn't skedaddle on me. I looked out over the valley. That way, if he glanced up, he'd see me unconcerned.

What price would we have to pay, trying to herd wheels over three states of unknown roads just to see a few smelly Eskimos and some savages eating puppies? Chances were more than good we'd

Victor McDaniel and Ray Francisco on the morning of their departure. Photograph courtesy of *Santa Rosa Press Democrat*

never make it up there, at least in time to see the fair, but I couldn't let Ray sniff a hint of my doubts.

In the west the sun slipped behind the last layer of oak-stubbled hill. Dusk would now go quickly to dark. Under the rim of hill just pocketing the sun was home: Mama, Papa, my three sisters, and most of the people I'd ever known, except for Ray. I dropped my eyes, not wanting to see the rim glow disappear.

Ray panted close, tugged alongside, then cruised on past, around the wide turn, and freewheeled down the shaded east grade. I grabbed the bill of my cap, pulled it low and rode after him. The shoulder was bumpy, but the dust was thin, and the long, steady, downhill grade even. By late dusk we rolled into the valley, near Napa. Ahead, Ray's dark form swung easily side to side, and I pumped hard to catch up. "The ditch," I yelled. "Looks wide enough to bed down next to the fence." We leaned the bikes against the slope of the ditch. "Best chain 'em together," I said. We couldn't be more alone on a road we sure didn't know.

In the near dark, we laid out Mama's bread and the chicken that was left. Ray said, "Let's thank the Lord first, Vic." I'd never remember. During the day Ray probably said grace too, but I didn't hear him. Evenings were another matter.

"We thank You for this food. And we ask You to bless the journey Victor and I have begun. It is Your will I should travel beside my friend. But I'll need Your help, Lord. We'll both need it. Amen."

Later, as we lay rolled loosely in our blankets back to back in the bottom of the ditch, Ray's breathing came regularly. The air smelled of alfalfa, sweet and damp and grassy. Across the road, crickets chorused to the moon that lifted yellow over the east hills. Ray's faith was right for him. I had my own, more a faith in what I could do. Still there's times a man needs help. Ray's faith might be a good thing to have along on this trip.

Off somewhere a wagon clattered, and men's voices carried without words.

Next morning we rode with the wind. Like a hot bellows, it dried our sweat and left us rimed with salt. Twice we water-stopped at cattle ranches in the Napa hills, again in Fairfield, and the last time in Vacaville. Now, close to Winters, our canteens again swung light and empty. Out here in the flat valley heat rose in glossy waves. Sweat sluiced down my back and front but dried fast in the wind I made.

Ahead, Ray turned. "Rear tire losing air," he hollered, slowing, feet splayed to either side before he swung off.

"Don't give it too much in this heat." I pulled up as he unclamped his pump. Ray's eyes were white-circled, and his face looked flushed. He could be over-hot. Not a good thing out here without any water.

"Next ranch we'll water-stop," I said and swiped my bandanna across my forehead. Overhead a hen hawk angled onto an air current, its fringed wings near to motionless. Some ways down the road, a dray pulled a hay loader out from a field, crossed the road, then all but disappeared in a sea of grain. I leaned over to rub dust from the Veeder cyclometer mounted on my bike's fork. "Twenty-nine miles from Santa Rosa," I announced, as Ray bounced his rear tire on the dirt.

He led out. The road was straight as a pole, with swells so gentle you couldn't say for sure where up started and down quit. To the north, a windmill was tiny by some miles. Even if the ranch dry-farmed there'd be water for the house. By the time we turned in on the dusty driveway, a narrow road slicing through gray-green almond trees, the sun hovered over the west hills. The house, an eighth of a mile or so in, wanted paint. No flowers softened its square lines. We followed the drive around back where the barn, twice the size of the house, had been freshly whitewashed. Last year's crop must not have been good enough to buy paint. A brown and white dog dozed by the barn doors. Part collie, part hound, looked like. For sure, no part watch dog. Next to the barn, a raw-wood bunkhouse had a door at each end, and four small windows along the sides. The windmill, atop a tank house, was as freshly whitewashed as the barn. After every shift of air, the steel fins groaned to a stop, and the vane held true. To one side of the back steps a hand pump beckoned.

"I'll go ask." I propped my bike against the landing. Turning, I saw a big woman standing spraddle-legged as she leaned on a hayfork in the wide barn door.

"You fellows got business?" Her voice was husky.

Ray propped his bike next to mine, and we crossed the yard. Of about our mamas' years, the woman looked like she hadn't spent many of them enjoying herself. Her gray-streaked hair was loosed from somewhere in back and straggled down her face. Her dress was of a substantial brown cloth, its hem heavy with a border collected from the stalls she must have been cleaning.

I took off my cap. "I'm Victor McDaniel, ma'am. We're on a bicycle trip from Santa Rosa to the Seattle Exposition. Me and my friend, Ray."

He nodded, cap in his hand. "We'd like to use your water, missus. Wash up some. Fill our canteens, with your permission."

The woman squinted past us to the bikes. "No more to do than wheel? Use the water." She gripped the hayfork and lumbered back inside the barn. We tossed our caps on our heads and half ran to the pump. Water gushed warm, then cool, a glory to gulp down. We each manned the handle for the other, drinking, separating ourselves from dirt. Then, behind us, the back screen squeaked open.

A frail young woman near our age smiled as she held the screen ajar, one trim foot in a neatly buttoned shoe showing from under her dark skirt. She was plain-featured, but there was a prettiness about her, in her cornflower eyes and the way she inclined her head. Her hair was the color of pale butter in the late sun. "Would you stay for supper?"

"We'd be pleased," I said.

"Is it for you to invite, miss?" Ray nodded toward the barn, but his gaze never left the girl.

"We've plenty," she said and opened the screen.

"I'm not sure. . . ." Ray muttered to me, but he'd already taken the bottom stair.

"The old lady?"

He nodded.

Mouth-tingling vapors of meat and vegetables wafted out. "We can leave right after." I followed him.

The young woman led through a screen porch lined with shelves covered in gathered muslin that gapped in places to show row on row of fruit cans, the rosin-soldered kind my mother used. In the kitchen, she pointed to a large, round table. "Sit down, please. I'll ring for Mama." Then facing us square on, "You're Ray. And Vic. I heard you say your names."

We looked at each other, then sat at the table. Out in the porch the girl picked up a school-sized hand bell from an upended lug box by the door, stepped outside and gave the bell several throws. Back at the counter, she deftly filled water glasses from the dipper and bucket. Her walk had a slender grace within her long full skirt as she brought the glasses to the table.

"My name is Helen MacIntosh." The kitchen was sticky hot, but Helen didn't sweat. Her milk-white forehead breathed clean and dry.

"How do you do," we chorused.

"You are on a bicycle trip?"

"Our second day out," I said, and wished my smile were as engaging as Ray's. "We're going north to see the World's Fair in Seattle."

"The state of Washington? On wheels? Oh my." She looked unbelieving from Ray, to me, and back to Ray.

The screen door banged, and Helen glided to the wood range where she stirred one of the three pots steaming on the large six-holer.

Helen's mother bulked in the doorway, her frame filling it a good two-thirds. "Use the water, I said."

"I asked them to eat with us." Helen stirred faster.

The woman strode to the table and thudded herself down in the chair opposite Ray. She'd washed up and set her hair to rights, but there was no mistaking the soil still on her hem.

"We'll be off, ma'am," I sputtered. Ray nodded, and we stood up.

"Mama!" Helen objected, setting a filled plate in front of her mother and another before me. The girl's veins traced a delicate blue under the white skin of her wrists. "These men are on a long trip. And we have plenty."

Ray and I exchanged looks.

Mrs. MacIntosh jabbed a fork into a chunk of stew meat glowing with brown gravy. "They can take time from riding around to eat our supper. But not for chores?"

"Just tell us what and we'll be proud to do them, ma'am," I said.

Ray shifted foot to foot. "We'd like to help, ma'am."

Helen sat down and gestured us to sit too.

Mrs. MacIntosh looked at Ray, then me. "I have a good-sized ranch here. Had three men on the place to knock almonds. But they lit out."

Helen pushed a napkin-covered plate at Ray. "Fresh-baked bread."

He took a slice and passed the plate to me. He hadn't taken a bite yet, and I knew he was rassling out some kind of grace inside himself.

Mrs. MacIntosh chewed as she talked. "You fellows give me a hand, and I'll give you a dollar a day. Each. Sleep in the bunkhouse. Eat like this."

"The men are going to the fair, Mama. We can manage." Helen moved her food around on her plate, but ate little.

"*You* can manage. It's not the kitchen needs almond knockers." Mrs. MacIntosh wiped her mouth with the napkin, wadded it up and stuffed it under the edge of her plate.

"Well?"

"We'd like to help," I said. "But we can't stay. We'd be glad to chop wood or tend the animals."

"Like to eat. Just don't like to work. That it?"

"Mama, they *told* you. . . ."

"Yep. They do chores. No field work." Her broad fingertips drummed the table. "You boys had your fill of food. Guess you best start riding those wheels. Be off to your good times."

"Thank you." Ray glanced at Helen, but she only watched her plate. "It was very good food. Before we chop the wood or work in the barn, I'd like to talk to my friend out on the porch, if you don't mind."

"Mind?" Mrs. MacIntosh's laugh was dry. She pulled herself up then and left the kitchen by the far door.

On the porch Ray spoke low, talking close to my face, "A couple of women trying to run a farm by themselves. What you thinking of, Vic? We can't leave without giving 'em a day's hand." At times like this Ray seemed as tall as me, and his voice that of a full man's. "We might just as well work now, here, *before* the money's run out. Ends up the same. Could you sleep easy thinking about that slip of a Helen working the fields after she's finished up in the house?"

"So, that's it! It's Helen."

"Halter your voice!"

Softer, I said, "I feel sorry for her too, but mostly because of her mother." Suddenly I could imagine Ray playing the little reverend to a martyred cook with spun gold for hair, while our Seattle Exposition faded away to a bad idea.

"You've made the decisions to now, Vic. This one's mine. We help out tomorrow. Besides, we need the two dollars."

3

The *Press Democrat*'s team of cyclists—'bicycle bums' the boys style themselves—Ray Francisco and Victor McDaniel, en route from Santa Rosa to the Seattle Exposition, are having many interesting experiences. Their friends and readers of the *Press Democrat* are following them by the diary they keep and which they are sending at intervals en route in letter form to this paper.

". . . when a hot spell of weather is encountered it is our intention to travel at night and rest in the heat of the day. We will take it easy at first until we get hardened but expect to make fairly good time through the valleys as it will naturally be slower in the mountain districts."

THE *SANTA ROSA PRESS DEMOCRAT*

our cots end to end lined each long wall of the narrow bunkhouse. On the wall facing the house four small windows were propped out, but the air still smothered hot. Ray set the lamp down on a fifty-pound lug box.

"Time we let Finley know we got out of town." He dug the tablet out of his rucksack, and his pencil began to scratch.

I grunted and flopped on a cot covered with a moth-eaten gray blanket.

Next morning, after Helen's eggs and fried potatoes, Ray and I crossed the yard as Mrs. MacIntosh slogged out the door of the barn carrying a wooden maul and a couple of tarpaulins. We rushed up, and I grabbed the tarps. Ray took the maul.

"Those trees at the corner." She nodded toward the drive. "Spread the tarps underneath. I'll be along with another maul."

We set off and at the corner tree smoothed the canvas pieces under it carefully. Ray hefted the maul, testing the fit of the head, which was a cross-section of oak limb ringed with an iron strap. Mrs. MacIntosh strode around the house now with a maul slung over her shoulder. She yelled, "Overlap those tarps."

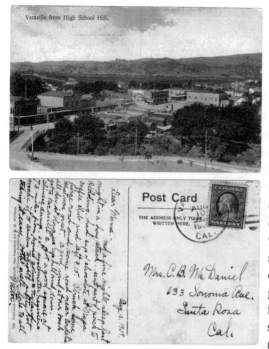

Vacaville from High School Hill.

Post Card

THE ADDRESS ONLY TO BE
WRITTEN HERE.

Mrs. C. B. McDaniel
633 Sonoma Ave.
Santa Rosa
Cal.

Quickly, we tugged one over the other by a few inches. "Ever knocked?"

We shook our heads as she reached us. "Use that, Vic." She gestured to Ray's maul, and he handed it to me. Then she slid the maul from her shoulder and pulled back. Her blow struck the trunk about waist level, and a hail of almonds peppered down. I ducked, but the rain of them was soft on my head and shoulders. Still in husks, they covered the canvas in a gray-green, furry mat. "Now you from your side," and she stood leaning on the maul. I raised back. The balance was different from an ax. Hard as I could, I hit the trunk. The report was louder than hers. The whole tree shook, but the fall was light.

"Save the tree! It's almonds we want!" She handed her maul to Ray. "Now the two of you. Opposite sides. Take turns. Get a rhythm going. Move around the tree. Probably have to circle a few times. Empty the tarps in the wagon." She pointed to a farm wagon, tongue down, two rows away. "Long poles next to it. Use 'em to get the inside branches." In a striding mass then, she was off toward the house.

It didn't take long to gauge the muscle behind the wallops, and she was right about the rhythm. There was even something satisfying about the crack-crack, crack-crack of wood on wood, his side, my side, blasting those nuts out of the tree. Once in the swing, we could reap a tree in two good turns. It was the drayage back to the wagon and the re-laying of the confounded tarps that was worth the dollars. Done with three rows, and two trees up on the next, we stopped to rest. Ray flipped the cover of his watch, the gold one his grandfather gave him. "Ten of twelve, Vic. We best go wash up for dinner."

Helen had fixed a fine beef soup and ham and mashed potatoes with a cream gravy as good as Mama's. Ray looked some foolish sitting across from Helen and making big eyes at her. In a shy and proper way, she was giving them back at him until, by the time she served the cherry pie, the two were ridiculously close to smitten.

Back in the orchard our strikes landed light and firm, bouncing off in recoil rather than pounding bruises into the trunk. My hit, Ray's, step left, my hit, his. The rhythm hypnotic let the mind drift off. I thought about the summers I worked for Luther Burbank in his rose garden across Santa Rosa Creek from our house. What an odd sight he was in his broad-brimmed hat pedaling home from his daily trip to the Post Office on his lady's bicycle, its basket full of mail. He'd tell me when I had dug holes deep enough for the roses. And at the planting of them, "Take care not to tear the outer skin," he'd warn me. "Disturbs the cambium. Cambium gives a plant its life." I never did know what the cambium was, but I hoped Ray and I hadn't disturbed it on these almond trees.

When we'd knocked the last tree in the third row and hauled and emptied the tarps into the wagon, Ray pulled out his watch. "Seven o'clock, railroad time. Supper at seven thirty."

At breakfast next morning, Helen told us her mother was already out cleaning horse stalls. "Says to tell you the mauls and tarps are just inside the barn."

Ray surprised me then by being the one to tell Helen what we'd decided, that we couldn't stay to work a second day. She looked up from her plate, eyes bright with glisten, and held Ray's gaze across the table. For longer than needed. "I was fixing chicken and dumplings," was all she said.

"Our yesterday's work could never pay for the good cooking we've already had, Helen," Ray told her. "We just hope we helped a little with the world of work you and your mama have here on the place."

By jingo, was he going to donate our two dollars? I pushed back my chair and shot him a look meant to burst that love bubble he was swimming around in. But he and Helen just sat, looking stunned at each other.

"Lawsy me, off to the A.Y.P.E.," I sing-songed, rousing Ray to his feet.

"I hope you'll pass this way on your trip home," said Helen, seeing us to the door. "I'd surely like to hear about that fair. With the farm work and all, I don't expect ever to leave the place except for supplies. But I have surely liked meeting you nice young men. And I so much like knowing you'll see those far-away places."

Ray loitered with her before following me out to the wheels. Even then, grabbing the handlebars till his knuckles whitened, he watched over his shoulder the screen door Helen had closed after us. We pushed around the corner of the house onto the dusty drive through the orchard, and I said, "You just gave those women our earnings, Ray."

"We can do without the money. They need it more than we do."

Our tires crunched in the thick dust. The only other sounds were the clangs in my head and the coarse yammer of a jay in a nearby tree. Then, behind us, Helen called, "Ray! Vic! Wait!"

Out the drive she ran to us. Dust rose about her small feet when she nearly skidded in her stop, breathless. "Here. The money Mama owes you. She says thank you for the help."

Helen shoved two silver dollars into Ray's hand. Then, from the great pocket of her print apron, she pulled out a loosely wrapped bundle that smelled of fresh-baked bread.

"Vic, you'll be hungry before you get far."

"Thank you," I said and took it.

"Oh, and here." From her other pocket what did she draw out but our dratted billiken. It was too embarrassing, grown men on a daring journey carrying around a clay doll.

"The little fellow was on the table when I cleared just now. You must have forgotten to pick it up." She smiled at Ray, the grinning figure nestled in her palm. He seemed reluctant to take it, but then reached for the God of Things That Ought to Be. "Thank you, Helen." She took his hand and folded his fingers around that idiot billiken, using a heap of time at it. Abruptly then, as in a powerful wrench of the will, she turned away, head bent, and walked quickly back toward the house.

Ray, eyes front, jammed the billiken into the end of his bedroll and, in a fearful hurry, pushed out. Catching up, I said—not asking really—"You didn't forget to pick that billiken up, now did you?"

But all the energy it might take for him to answer was used up in his glassy stare straight out ahead.

4

❀ ❀ ❀

Good, level, watered and oiled roads all the way. Passed some
fruit ranches, but mostly alfalfa and grain fields which stretch
farther than the eye can see.

FROM THEIR LETTER TO THE *SANTA ROSA PRESS DEMOCRAT*

Yee-ow!" I took both hands off the bars to shoot them skyward
and bellowed, "See-attle!" Ray jerked a look at me over his
shoulder, weaved a little, then turned forward. Too much of a
minister to let out his gladness, I thought. Only in the back of my
head could I allow that the gleeful part of Ray might still be
smothered in an ache for Helen.

Full of peaches we'd picked up and Helen's package of bread and
fried potatoes and sausage, I was as pleased as those saucy
meadowlarks belting away in the grain fields. That fair might hold
still long enough yet for us to see the swaying hips of those dancers
in the Streets-of-Cairo show. And maybe get our picture taken in
one of those new automobiles.

The road level and watered, miles greased under us. Heat
hammered down heavy, but our speed turned the lazy air into wind
that cooled. Push, let up, push. Rhythm was good; wheels sang on
the baked, packed dirt. My load was light as goose fluff, and the
numerals on the Veeder box whizzed around; one hundred miles
from home. I shoved my goggles up to let the sweat dry, but the
bugs buck-shotted my eyes, and I pulled them back down.

The bike seemed to skim faster than when I raced in Henry
Jenkins' Bike Shop Run, the time I won the Bundy carbide lamp
whose nickel-plated brass lines now gleamed between my
handlebars. In his second race I'd won the brass bell with the
embossed serpent and wished it had been another lamp so Ray
would have a new one too. But when I gave him the bell, he said it
would be a jaunty way to answer my police whistle and his old arc
light would do him fine. I fingered the cord around my neck and
the whistle that hung from it. The bell and whistle were our signal

system. We hadn't used it yet, but we knew the long and short toot talk of the locomotives so we could communicate over a distance. A single short: apply brakes, stop. Double long: release brakes, proceed. The system could be important in hill country; the lead man coming on a team or rig could signal the man behind.

Lead man. I looked ahead for Ray. The level, straight road shimmered empty. I stood on the brakes and tried to remember when I'd last seen him. Must have been when we flew through Yolo, that last smudge of a town. I swung off. A water wagon and team of two crossed the road toward a steam-engined threshing machine pounding away in the field. Ray could have tumbled, rolled off in the ditch.

Heart thudding, my eyes probed both ditches, the walls of bending grass. I poked the whistle in my mouth, then saw him. Across the road he pushed his wheels up out of a gravelly creek bed.

"Nature stop!" he hollered.

I pedaled up. "Just had one. What's wrong?"

"Maybe the fruit. Insides feel like a boiler works." He laid his bike down and took off at a gallop to squat behind some scrags of grass. Underway again, we rode side by side. "We'll buy you something at the next stop. "Lord knows you don't need the Orino laxative fruit syrup Mama stuck in my sack. To her the only problem's the other way 'round." Ray smiled, but his color was blotchy, and his sweat bubbled. If he couldn't stay in the saddle, that Alaska-Yukon-Pacific Exposition would never set eyes on these two Santa Rosa galoots.

The town of Blacks was several houses, a smithy shop, wagon repair, and general store where we leaned our bikes. The puffy-faced fellow behind the glass display case told us, "Cardui's dollar a bottle. I'll give it to you for ninety-eight cents."

Ray dug in his pocket and jangled Mrs. MacIntosh's silver dollar on the glass top.

"For that could you throw in some tins? Baked beans, corn?" I asked.

"Ten cents a tin." He looked over my right shoulder, not at me.

I tossed three dimes beside the dollar, and the fellow picked up the money with the shaky hands of a man too used to drink. Outside, Ray swallowed what we thought was a dose and made a face. "Worse than Brother Benjamin's Herbalo." He nodded toward the window. Inside, the storekeeper on a ladder reached to a high shelf and brought down a bottle. "Let's shove out," I said. Best we get on the road before Ray had an itch to minister.

Just out of town he threw up the tonic, along with everything else. "We've done better than thirty miles today," I said. "Time for camp."

"We circled Dunnigan on the map. I can make it."

We rode slow for the three miles, while the orange sun squashed itself on the distant west hills. Ray looked pale and unsteady. I stifled my wonder about whether it was lost love as much as strong sun that had unhorsed him. Side by side, we pedaled down Dunnigan's main street. Chairs on the board sidewalks lined both sides. In straight-backs and rockers, men sat laughing and talking, a cigar or chaw or pipe in most every mouth. At this hour outside was cooler than in. The talk stopped as we passed, and I was glad Ray didn't pick this time to topple.

Out of town, we aimed for the first haystack, and he was asleep before I could open the tin of beans.

5

❋ ❋ ❋

The *Press Democrat* Monday night received another
interesting letter from Ray Francisco and Victor McDaniel, the
Santa Rosa boys who are riding their bicycles from Santa Rosa
to Seattle. . . . details of the trip will be read with much
interest by their Santa Rosa friends. The letter follows: "We
made Dunnigan . . . lots of hay in that country and we made
use of it that night."

FROM THEIR LETTER TO THE *SANTA ROSA PRESS DEMOCRAT*

My dreams of Helen holding the billiken and Mrs. MacIntosh with a maul over her shoulder dragged along like a worry I couldn't name, and were shot through with how would we buy Ray a rail ticket home if he were too sick to wheel, and could I make the trip to Seattle alone? When I woke up, the day was well on. The shadow of the haystack had even shortened. Ray still slept where he'd thrown himself last night.

One jump and I was on the ground. The bicycles leaned into the stack where I'd chained them together, tires plump, side bags bulging properly. With my jack knife I cut the top from the tin of corn. Friday, the thirteenth, and Ray too weak to travel; it made a man consider. Our stack must belong to the farm just past the railroad station and loading dock. If the farmer did see us, he would be sure we were hobos and probably not run us off.

I unhooked the tin cup from my belt, filled it with creamed corn and hunkered at the base of the stack. A field mouse skittered in front of me, stopped still as stone, then streaked off. Squinting into the sun, I saw another motion. In a billow of dust a mule team and wagon slogged toward the loading dock at the train station. Behind that assembly was another, and could be another behind it, but the dust was too thick for sureness.

Ray sat up, the sun bright on him.

"Creamed corn?" I held out my cup for him to look into.

"That and most anything else."

I tossed him a smile and poured corn into his cup. But one gulp and he set the cup in the hay beside him and lay back. "I'll maybe take it easy here for an hour or so, Vic."

"Too hot to travel anyway. Sleep. I'll get on over to the station there. Fill us up on water." I slung the canteens over my shoulder.

Ray dug in his pocket and handed me his gold watch. "Set it by station time."

In the dock yard a twelve-mule team and dead-axle wagon had pulled to position alongside the loading platform, animals and wagon all made of dust crusted on thick. As the skinner slid from the back of the wheeler mule, all twenty-four ears swiveled toward him. His sliding off must be part of the language between skinner and team. I swung myself up to sit on the dock and watch.

The skinner walked the length of his train, tugged at a strap here, adjusted a buckle there, worked on the connection between the lead span.

"Jockey-stick must have twisted."

I jumped up and whirled at the voice behind me. Canteens clanked to the boards.

"Hold on there." The man was about my height, around thirty, his pinstripe shirt and string tie showing him to be from the city. "Thought you saw me come up." His smile was one-sided, and he talked from the corner of his mouth.

Lifting his flat-topped boater, he mopped his brow with a shirtsleeve.

"Guess I was watching the team," I said, hoping it didn't sound like an apology, and picked up the canteens.

"Hang around here you'll learn more than mules." The man's mustache quivered before he smiled. "Skinners' tongues'll peel the hide right off your ears." He drew two Blaine cigars from his shirt pocket and held one out.

"No, thanks," I said and turned to watch the skinner stoop and peer at the draw chain between the two rows of animals.

"Mules are smarter than most folks you'll ever know." The pinstriped fellow closed the distance I'd put between us. "Skinner's wise to his animals. Won't stand for no double shuffles. But those mule devils are smart. Catch on to jerk line palaver quicker'n boys take to cussin'."

This man talked too much. I bent forward to try to hear what the skinner was saying so softly to the lead span.

"Smartest span is up at lead," the dandy went on. "Nigh lead tells his partner through that jockey stick what the skinner told 'em to do. Smart." This queer potato sidled too close, and I sat back down on the platform, away from his face and his smoke.

"Hit that collar, you unholy bastards!" the skinner bellowed. The mules tested the load, then plodded slowly forward.

"You trampin' to 'Frisco?" The pinstriper sat down next to me, puffing on that stogie.

I inched away. "Wheel trampin', not train trampin'."

"Yeah? Don't see your bicycle." He looked around.

"Out in the hayfield," I said, then wondered why I told him.

"Stacks are fine bedding down all right. I'd say you're better off on wheels than rails. Fellas running the trains these days are mighty picky-minded. Lines out of 'Frisco, Kansas country, none hold with folks doin' other sorts of business. Ordinary men like you and me, they're quick to chuck us out. Bicycle, now that's a smart one."

This guy was probably a bad-hat that got booted off a train. I stood up. As I did, Ray's watch fell to the ground, a long drop from where I stood on the platform. Deep in my pants pocket, it never could have fallen without help. This slippery fellow had been about to light-finger the watch! Cozying up, he must have been working it out. On his feet now too, he eyed me with that sideways grin. Did he think I was so young, so foolish, I couldn't figure him? The shifty, thieving. . . .

I came at him, rammed a fist to his gut, another at his jaw. But he turned. My blow glanced, didn't double him. He spun half around, yellow, gutless, his back to me. Whirling, his leg shot out and up, the heel of his pointy-toed shoe missing my groin by inches to catch my thigh. I lurched to the side and pitched forward. Watching me over his shoulder, he backed closer. Then his elbow a firebolt cut sharp at my cheek and smashed my nose. Crunch and pain filled my ears and eyes as I went down. I lay there sick. Flattened by a no-good sharpie, my face mushed, my head scrambled.

"The kid's addled," he was saying to the dockhands gathering around.

I turned on my side. Blood was wet on my shirtfront and puddled the boards under me. I labored to my knees, pain pounding in my nose and jaw, the flesh of my face feeling loose. I anchored a foot under me. A dockhand said, "He'll be fine," and drifted away with the others.

I untied my bandanna from around my neck and put it to my nose. Carefully, I let myself over the side of the dock, picked the watch out of the dust and held it to my ear. Nothing. But Ray hadn't wound it.

No sign of the pinstriped snake, only the next twelve-mule assembly snorting, clanking and rattling into position beside the dock. Outside the station, the cold water of the pump slowed my bleeding. I rinsed my shirt and bandanna, filled the canteens and set the watch by the clock through the station window, then headed out for the long walk to the stack.

Ray was asleep in the small shade of the north side. I slumped into what was left, but not before I'd draped a leg over both bikes.

"Victor!" Ray was shaking my shoulders.

I struggled, wished he'd go away. The sun was down.

"What happened? You been fighting?"

I moved my head. Everything hurt. A hand to my nose, I sat up slowly. "Had to, Ray." My head thrummed; my nose ached fire. Nodding, he poured water on his bandanna and told me to hold it to my nose. "Breeze on the wet cloth will keep down the swelling."

The dry evening smelled of warm hay; my nose still had life. Then it hit me. "Can't camp in these stacks, Ray. There's a two-bit scallywag's sure to come worming around to make off with our wheels."

"Bent up as you are, we couldn't even make Arbuckle."

"Doesn't have to be far. We just can't stay here."

Less than two hours later we were bedded down under tall eucalyptus trees, me sleeping by fits and starts, the trees' menthol odor working its way into my throbbing head. Bark scales crackled under me when I turned, but I found no comfortable spot. Off somewhere a coyote barked. Another howled in answer.

Ray's breathing was regular. He'd eaten and kept it; whole again. This day was lost, and we'd likely not get far tomorrow. We'd lolled in this Sacramento Valley over long. I moaned. Should have killed that filthy jack-a-dandy.

6

❀　❀　❀

We're near Corning, Mama. Had big meals at farmhouses. All the rich milk we could drink. They won't take any money for it. Will write a long letter soon. I still weigh 160 pounds. Victor.

FROM A PENNY POSTCARD

Through the heat and the wheat we made Arbuckle and Williams on Saturday. Barely seventeen miles, but in the right direction. We water-stopped at two farms where the women insisted we eat and rest. We did look a miserable pair, I guess, Ray peering out of his hollow eyes and my face the color of vulture meat. But they said it was fine the way we wolfed their food.

The country outside Williams was as flat as the town. But the ditch by the road was scooped enough we didn't lump on the landscape once we bedded down, and we slept the night through, even with the trains rattling and clanging not thirty feet away. When the eastern sky began to pale a light green above the Sierra Nevadas, the ants got to biting and I sat up. Over the gray flanks of the foothills to the northeast bloomed a pink cone: Mt. Lassen, the mountain folks said would someday erupt. Farther north in the dim distance, the broad peak of Mt. Shasta, right where our map said it should be.

I laid a hand on Ray's back. "It's Sunday, old pal. But we have a day's labor all the same."

Sitting up, his eyes moved to our bikes against the side of the ditch. "You got a flat, Vic." He slapped at the ants crawling on his cheek and ear. While I worked at the tire, Ray poured water from his canteen and splashed his face. Morning was hardly born, and already the heat sat heavy. I swiped a sleeve across my forehead and snapped the pump back in place. "Want to eat at a wagon in Maxwell?"

"Fried eggs and potatoes?" He took a pull from his canteen and screwed the cap back on. Shooting his arm out like a rifle, he cried, "Charge!" and was Teddy Roosevelt.

The surface was the best, oiled, level, fast. In the lead, Ray pedaled strong, and my face felt back in shape, even with the road jolts. Maxwell had no lunch wagon, but a man and his wife walking to church directed us to a widow's place with a sign in the window saying lodging and meals. Here a round-faced woman charged us thirty-five cents but served up biscuits, as many as we could eat, and strawberry jam with the eggs and potatoes. After we'd eaten and had unlocked the padlock on the bicycles' chain, Ray put a hand on my arm. "Let's give thanks to the Lord, Vic," and bent his head. I bent mine and belched softly.

MT. LASSEN, NEAR RED BLUFF, CAL.

Out of town the heat now had a firm grip. My sweat poured. Sun shimmering on the grain tassels to either side of the road was a trial for the eyes. Even the birds were quiet. But up there ahead Ray's strength was holding.

By mid-afternoon, in Willows we found a bench under an oak where we drank water and slept. In the worst of the heat we'd traveled nearly twenty-five miles. Now, as the day cooled we'd manage more, and shoved out.

After town, farms and houses were scarce. Even the railroad left us to travel parallel half a mile away. Groves of eucalyptus gave way to an occasional olive orchard and a few scattered oaks. The sun was low now but still burned. My canteen had been empty for some bit of time. I hollered up, "You dry yet?" Ray shook his capless canteen upside down. "A mile back." But the roads were smooth and lately sprinkled. We'd soon find a house and water. Abruptly though, the country took on an unfamiliar cast. The ground rolled in swells so gentle as not to be there, giving lie to distance. Lassen and Shasta ducked in and out of view and never seemed to change size. As we crossed the board bridges water in the wide, gravelly beds trickled brackish and poisonous-looking. Finally, at the end of a long, poplar-lined drive a cluster of planted trees shifted in a changing air current. Ray turned in and I followed. Dismounting, we walked our bikes through the deep dust. But at the end of the drive we found only the charred remains of a building and the carbon-colored cement of a cellar overgrown with grass and straggly rose-bushes. A large shrub squeaked as it scraped against the still-standing, blackened chimney.

Close to a whisper, Ray said, "They'd have had water."

Buried in a tangle of grass and old boards, we found the well. Six or seven feet down, a water crock was lodged in a thicket of growth, the rope that once suspended it gone. Inside the crock was a murky oily liquid, butter from another time.

"Nothing fit to drink, even if we could get at it," I said, the words returning eerie and hollow from the well.

Back on the road, my legs quivered and my chest hurt. Ray would be feeling weakened too, but he was too crusted with dirt and sweat to tell if his color was sick.

"Corning should come soon, Vic," he hollered back, as if he fancied now to be the strong one. So I didn't answer him.

As ever, the ground moved steadily backward under my wheels. My legs pedaled same as always, but seemed somehow separate from me. Of a sudden I knew I should give a blast of my whistle to Ray up there, but I needed both hands to steady as I braked. I didn't fall. I jumped from the bike as it toppled, stumbled into an oak and fell into the ditch. Here the sun had already set, and all was black.

❈

"Come on, Vic. *Vic!*" A cool, sweet liquid bathed my cracked lips, and I ran my tongue over them. "Easy," Ray said, squeezing moisture from his bandanna, as he crouched over me. Tomato juice, wet and wonderful.

Slowly I sat up, but grabbed my shoulder. Bleeding. Must have landed on it. I could move it though, thank the good Lord. My wheel lay all wamper-jawed on the far side of the ditch. Ray put a hand on my arm. "Bike's okay." He poured another fat tomato in my cup, the yellow strip of sealing wax still clinging to the edge of the tin's lid. "Mama's tomatoes. Be glad to shed the weight. We'll bed down here in the ditch."

Me the leader of us since third grade, and he tells where we should bed down. I started to stand up to argue, but wobbled and sank back down. Later, my body glad to be flat out, and my mind easy because my bike frame was still true, I watched a flock of swallows dip and turn, making their rusted-axle squeaks in the bottle-green sky.

Next day was even hotter, but my legs remembered their job, and my shoulder was only an ache and a bruise. The town of Corning lay just over the rise from where we'd camped. In the general store we bought bread and cheese, a tin of corned beef, and patching cement. Canteens heavy again, we rode north out of town.

A small shout ahead, Ray swayed side to side between walls of drab-green olive orchards. The freshly oiled road was slow going. Tires tugged up from the gummy surface tar-coated, raisined with gravel. They shot inky hot bits at my pants and shirt, sticking fast, burning my skin through the cloth.

I bent to read the Veeder: two hundred eleven miles. One week from Santa Rosa, one dollar seventy-four cents in our purse, four weeks of travel ahead, and about three weeks of work for enough money to get us through. A total of seven weeks, one past October 1 when the Seattle newspaper would hand us twenty-five dollars, if we were there to hand them to.

Ahead, slugging up a short rise, Ray stood on the pedals too, his back, legs, shoulders looking more fit than I ever thought they could. He might rile me, but mostly I liked him, the way his mind worked through an idea to its end, and the way he was strong inside himself, not just outside with his body like me. I wondered if he was on this trip so I wouldn't have to go alone. Ray was one to do that sort of thing.

Just south of Redding we camped early so we could set to work scraping the gummed-up oil and gravel from our tires and duffel. Off to the east Mt. Lassen was a rosy pyramid in the late light; golden Shasta compassed north. Enough glow was left to write Mama and Papa while Ray took the rifle to find us a squirrel for supper.

"We are making good time," I wrote, never mentioning that our chances of getting to the fair in time were now sadly slim.

7

Between Anderson and Redding we passed over some of the
best road we have struck so far. As a whole, we have found
good roads all along the valley, but they look pretty rough
from here on. The Siskiyou mountains are now staring us in
the face, and we are living in anticipation of some fine trout
fries during the coming week.

FROM THEIR LETTER TO THE *SANTA ROSA PRESS DEMOCRAT*

At Redding's general store we bought some hard candy and a
jar of Vaseline for Ray to use to pack the coaster brakes. Our
mouths full, we walked the bikes back a block to the city
park where we took them apart. Ray cleaned and oiled, lingering on
every detail to give the wheels a better than usual service.

Ray Francisco on the free bridge north
of Redding, California.

Mountains would exact their cost,
even with his care. Lunch was a tin
of beef and a few plums before we
pedaled out of town.

In the middle of the long free
bridge across the Sacramento River
we propped our wheels against the
diamond-patterned metal side rail
and leaned over to watch the heavy
water travel with surprising speed.

On the north side, pedaling was
an effort through dust that spewed
up thick and red. But around the
first turn the tires bounced
something fierce on the rocks
beneath the dust, so we got off and
pushed. Shasta was higher and fuller now. Mountains hemmed us
three sides around: Siskiyous to the north, Sierras, east, Trinities,
west. No way out now but back or up. Fair or no fair, we were
committed to this lonely country with its blood-colored dirt and its
roads fit only for Miller and Lux cattle.

At a crest I mounted and kept my seat all the way down the grade, but about lost my insides for the thumping. Reaching the bottom I stopped alongside Ray. We took pulls on our canteens as we looked about for a signboard saying Dunsmuir. One road hairpinned to the left; another just as ugly switched right. Ray jerked his head toward the left and slung his canteen over a shoulder. "Road probably skirts the hill then swings north."

"One to the right's already going north," I said, the decision-maker, and turned onto it. But after half an hour of mostly walking the bikes up a draw, we came to the end of the road at a deserted shack among a few misshapen digger pines and a litter of empty store cans and broken bottles.

The roof of the slapdash cabin had given up; daylight blotched the inside. An old rocking chair lodged crazy-angled on the broken porch, one of its rockers punched through the rotten boards. Hanging motionless from an uncut roof support was a scruffy coyote hide, the fur gone from it in dollar-sized patches. Next to the building, a lizard sunned itself on the rounded wood of an old pick handle that lay in the dirt beside a granite-ware coffee pot, its bottom rusted out. The lizard's scaly dry body looked part of the wood, and his bb-shot eyes fixed on us. Then, quick as a star falling, he darted off the handle through the dust to disappear under the coffee pot.

"Should have taken that left road," I allowed, flipping off my cap to mop my forehead.

"I don't see the water," he said, face flushed.

"Canteen empty?"

"Half full." He sloshed it.

"Could have been a dry camp. Winter and spring maybe there's. . ." I didn't finish, to better watch a jackrabbit scuttle through the scrub behind the shack. Ray saw him too. "I'll get us supper. No time to unwrap the rifle." He worked at the strap of my bag, the one that held the revolver.

"Caliber's too big," I warned. "Tag him. Don't pulverize him."

He pulled out the gun just as old mister rabbit hopped around the corner, bouncing this way and that up the hill before stopping under a manzanita. In a flick the jack set sail, a dun-drab streak on a zigzag course but for the now and again wild jump high enough to survey terrain. I scrambled after Ray fast as I could, dodging boards, rocks, brush, to keep him in sight. Looking right, left, gun held slack, he started toward a prospector's hole in the face of the hill, its wheelbarrow-sized entrance clogged with dirt and fallen timbers.

"Lost him?" I hollered.

"Little rascal's close by," he yelled.

Then, as struck by a freight, Ray's leg kicked straight out. He howled, fell back, and was down. The gun blasted wild and dropped. I ran to him.

"Grab it! Pull it out!"

My God! A snake big as my arm flailed over Ray as he lay flat on his back. Its body thrashed in thick curls, slapped the ground, hit a rock. The head of it was caught in Ray's trouser leg. I grabbed for its writhing middle, but it wriggled away. The rattler hurled heavy twists, but I had it now. It thrashed free. In a frenzy, it pounded Ray's knee, slammed my legs, whipped my ankle. I grabbed, got a grip near the head, and yanked. The fangs stayed hooked in the cloth. I worked my grip back, fighting the thick body with every muscle I had. I grabbed for the middle, the tail banging my back, my head. With the strength of a horse, it surged away, but I had a hold again, wrestling its awful power to tug the scaly, muscled mass from Ray's leg. But the head was still caught, fangs locked fast in the cloth of his pants.

Suddenly, between the head and where I grabbed, loomed the snubbed barrel of the revolver. The air exploded! My head, insides, burst with sound. I fell back, the churning body still in my grip. But the snake was loose from Ray, from his pants. Blood drenched the shredded meat and bone piece of the snake I held. "My God, Ray!" I threw it down the hill as far as I could.

A wisp of smoke curled from the barrel of the Iver-Johnson in his hand. He looked down at his leg and the rattler's head and a foot-long stub of snake twisting there, still fastened to his trouser. "Better cut the thing out, Vic." He laid the gun in his lap and reached in a back pocket. "Fish knife," and handed it to me.

I took hold of the snake piece near the head. The rattler was shedding its skin. Already it had started to peel away from the upper jaw. The head was half in, half out of the old skin. Blinded by the cast-off film over its eyes, the snake couldn't see. It would strike at anything, and without its usual warning rattle.

Hands steady, Ray held the pants leg taut. "Don't think he got me. But I'm not sure." I kept a snug pull on the snake-head and cut. Up from the cuff, past those lethal fangs. Faster, move faster. Don't touch those fangs. At last, down to the cuff. I slung the whole mess, snake and cloth, out in the brush.

He pulled the pant leg high, and we examined the skin, ankle to knee, every freckle, hair. He pushed the flesh of his calf one way and the other, turned his knee out, in. No double pricks of red. No scratch or hole or dread twin dots.

On my haunches, I sat gasping. "You're not bit!" Then I jumped up wild and mostly idiot. "Not bit—!" But I eased down to sit beside him, my head on rollers. Low in my stomach a flutter rose. Was I going to cry? Grabbing Ray, I couldn't let go. We sat holding to one another, and I sobbed. Sickness welled up in me then, and I let him go.

On my hands and knees, the vomit came.

"Poor Victor." Ray's hand was on my back.

I didn't raise my head, but kept the position to be certain I'd done it all.

"Don't like saying this, hoss," his voice was gentle.

"But snakes mostly don't travel single. This one's companion could be close by. Let's be getting on back."

A chill took me, toes to fingers. I staggered to my feet. If I had to vomit, I'd do it on the way to the bottom. "Good idea," I said, calm as I could. But Ray beside me was pale as hawk fodder. He was the one should sit awhile, but not now.

Then the rabbit, that cheeky little cause of it all, came lippity-lopping out from the brush below the mine entrance. In a kind of madness he short-circled ten feet or so ahead of us, cut sharp and disappeared beneath the broken timbers of the mine hole. Eyes ranging left, right, we made our slow way down the hill.

At the bottom, near the corner of the shack, Ray stooped to pick up a length of light rope, frayed but of a piece. "Could be handy." Then he slumped. Head between his legs, his shoulders shuddered, and he shook all over. Quickly I wrapped my body around him, as much as I could with him all bunched up. He felt cool, and terror gripped me. Ray might die. People did die from a bad fright. Even if he wasn't bit, he could die. His skin was going cooler. I pulled his head up. His eyes were closed, his tan face yellow, trembled. "Ray! You hear me?"

Where was his God? He better help out quick. To straighten Ray out would cool him even more. I laid my head on his back, the ache in me big as the world.

After awhile, maybe a long while, he didn't shake anymore. He began to feel warmer. My arms stiff around him, I shifted my legs to sit down. He raised his head then and opened his eyes, but closed them again. At last he said, "I'm rested." Shakily, he got to his feet, then planted them firmly apart.

A stranger to myself, my fears turned of a sudden to defiance. "We don't know these mountains, Ray. There's no farms to get water, no roads we can make time on, can't even find the right ones. We'll be soon out of money. And there's nothing here but rattlesnakes and no telling what else. If one of us gets bad hurt. . . " I kicked the dirt. "I'm for going back. We can't make it to the fair in time anyhow."

Ray was at the canvas bag snugging the revolver down and the rope in after it. "We could get just as hurt going back as forwards." His voice was thin. "We could work for more money before we cross the mountains. That way we'd know better how much travel time we have left."

"We know now. Not time enough to push bikes through three states and work too. We go back." My middle had a flop and flutter. I could throw up again. "Besides, you might get sick if we travel too hard."

He lifted the flap of his backpack, pulled out his small Bible and wedged it down his pants pocket. "I'll be fine." He slipped the pack straps over his shoulders and mounted. I followed, grateful for the downhill, feeling testy at Ray, myself, at Santa Rosa folks for backing us in such a foolish venture.

8

Left Redding by the free bridge and found poor roads and a great many hills to start with. We got off of the main road four times during the day as there were no signs to guide us, and the roads ran in every direction. We passed over grade after grade before we reached the Pit River.

FROM THEIR LETTER TO THE *SANTA ROSA PRESS DEMOCRAT*

The sun jerked me awake, mirrored as it was from the solitary window of the ferryman's cabin across the water. Against the steady throb of the river I heard the whinny of a horse and clatter of wheels. Ray, hunkered at a small fire, held over it three sizzling trout bracketed by crossed sticks. "Seems snake handling brings a man easy sleep," he teased.

"You should have kicked me awake," I said, annoyed, embarrassed. So I made a show of watching the opposite shore where a nervous bay neighed as it drew a wagon up onto the ramp of the raft-like ferry. The redheaded ferryman drew on one of two long ropes at either end of the boat. These were pullied to the cable that was stretched high above the river. As he shortened the rope to our side, the pully setting up a howl and screech, the boat canted slantwise. Current took it right away, moving the boxy craft crablike but at a respectable rate, across the water. Maybe fourteen feet wide and twenty or so long, the reaction ferry, at an angle to the flow, stayed on a straight course, the water powering it piling up and eddying around the corners. Nearer, the ferryman and his passenger raised their hands and smiled at us. I did the same, as I tied my blanket on the bike. Ray nodded and turned back to pulling the cooked fish from the sticks.

On our side of the river now the ferryman lowered the ramp, landing it on the bank with a dull thump. The bay clacked down the boards, and the old man on the wagon seat hollered to the ferryman, "Bradwell, get an Electro-Life for those piles. My cousin sits comfortable for the first time in twenty years." And he bounced up the hill.

Bradwell yelled something back as he carried a mooring rope ashore and threw it around the trunk of a pine. After securing it in a bowline, he sauntered over to us, the split of his smile showing teeth brindled by tobacco. "Traveling far?"

"Aiming for Seattle," I said. "We hope to take in that fair."

"Those wheels see you all the way there?"

"They better."

Bradwell squatted to put a giant cone on the spent fire. The sun now cast fingers of light on our side of the river, finding the ferryman's carrot-red hair that tumbled from under his mash of a hat in fierce, tight curls. The man's lively blue eyes took in Ray, the fish, me. "I'll hope with ya," he said and stood up.

When we'd introduced ourselves all around, Bradwell pounded down his hat. "I'll be off. Make the crossing. Come back for you after we've had breakfast."

"There's fish enough for three," Ray offered.

"Thanks, but I'll be having my oatmeal." He stuck a forefinger in one cheek, pulled out a tobacco wad and snapped it into the fire where it hissed. Then he spat a brown arc, watched till it hit the river shallows, and was off. At the pine he worked loose the bowline and dashed up the planks onto the ferry. Soon water built against the upstream side, and the howl of the pulley wheel peeled my ears.

Ray and I ate all three trout, the wrinkles of my stomach at last bulging taut. I said, "Must be a lonely life living in a cabin at the bottom of a river canyon, only an occasional traveler to talk to."

"Man likely savors his own company, that and a river talking soft at him through the night."

Soon, without our seeing him push out, Bradwell's raft of a ferry angled into the current on its way across to us. Sun played sparkles on the froth of water buildup and fired glints in the ferryman's hair. Packed and ready, we pushed up the ramp and to the middle of the ferry. Bradwell pulled hand over hand on the draw rope, saying, "You men think this pulley screams? Camp in these parts and you'll hear worse. Mountain lion scream sounds like a she-lady in mortal trouble, and there's lions here all right. Wolves, bear, elk. Elk with the biggest antlers are mostly north and east of the Shasta Mountain."

Over the squeal of the pulley, Ray said, "Fine country. Animals are proper. What do we owe you, Mr. Bradwell?"

"Twenty-five cents. For two and wheels."

Ray ran an arm down his bedroll.

"There's times animals aren't the big worry in these parts," Bradwell went on, as the boat straightened and we were smoothly on our way. "In the 'fifties, Indians decided to take this country back. Dug pits, covered 'em with leaves, sticks. On the bottom put elk antlers, point side up. Marched folks over those pits. Left 'em down there to die." Bradwell's head dropped to his chest for a moment. Raising it, he said, "Pits took care of their own law breakers too. Only mister grizzly got hauled out if he fell in. Indians storied that grizzly was their father. Pits, they're still around. Indians, the river, named for 'em."

After a rummage down that bedroll, Ray's hand finally pulled out our purse. But behind it, the billiken tumbled to the planks. Bradwell's gaze fell with it. "Patron spirit of the Seattle fair. Thought you hadn't been there yet." He looked suspicious.

Ray picked up the lump of clay. "We bought it at a road show from the fair."

"I'll take the billiken if you don't have money."

"We've got money," I assured him, and wondered about the stresses on that main cable. It would have to be mighty strong to hold the boat in the rise of spring water, and I was glad it was August.

Bradwell watched Ray stuff the silly figure back down the bedroll. "Billiken would do fine. Better than money, if the shuffle's the same."

Ray handed him the two-bit piece. "We'd like to keep the billiken, sir."

As we neared the north bank, weather lines smoothed in Bradwell's forehead, and his lips parted to show a smudged hint of teeth. Around the corner of his cabin I thought I glimpsed a flash of bright blue. His eyes saw mine. "My Mary."

I nodded. So Bradwell wasn't as lonely as we thought.

While he eased the ramp down, I stole another glance at the corner. There, peering around it, was the brown face of a young Indian woman. Bradwell watched me, mooring rope in his hand. Up the bank, circling the rope around a boulder, he called to her, "Come."

Ray and I pushed our bikes on to the road and stopped, not certain what Bradwell expected us to do. He ambled over then, his gaze on the girl, and almost whispered to us, "Little Bird Mary. Her father killed a grizzly north on the mountain. Came at 'em, and her daddy stopped it with a thirty-eight. But a man is punished for killing his father. Even if that father is a bear. By the time I come on 'em in the pit her father was dead, Mary most near. I nursed her back here. But she's forever afraid. Gets nervous when I'm on the other side for long." Louder, he called, "Come. Francisco. McDaniel." His hands were on our shoulders. "Little Bird Mary."

The girl walked to Bradwell, her black hair in a thick plait brought forward of her shoulder, her blue skirt falling in soft fullness. Slender and taller than most Indian women, she swung along with a strong grace, but her eyes were timid. Then I saw the bundle on her back.

Bradwell smiled, his eyes dancing back the blue of her skirt. "She won't let that baby out of her sight." He turned the girl gently around. Over the bindings the small head of the baby lolled to one side, asleep, ablaze with carrot-red hair. Bradwell reached down between the baby and the mother's back to pull out a slender cord about the child's neck. From the cord dangled a for-sure, God-of-Things-That-Ought-to-Be billiken. "Customer gave it for his crossing. Mary says it keeps away harm."

Little Bird Mary turned then, her doe-brown eyes more trusting, an easy, snowy smile opening her lovely face.

"For safe baby." Her voice was soft as wind in high pines. Not more than seventeen, she really was wildly pretty.

"Yes," I agreed, my voice the clatter of wheels on planks. Only then I noticed Mary was early-on pregnant. So that was it. Bradwell knew his Mary soon would need another protection around another little neck. I said, "Thanks for letting us meet your family, Bradwell. We'll send you another billiken from the fair."

As we pushed up the road, we turned to wave. Bradwell and Mary stood close, his muddy smile broad enough to bridge the river.

9

❀   ❀   ❀

Dear Alma,...we made our way up and down some rough grades to the United States Fishery on the McCloud River. Reaching this place at dark we wasted no time in making camp. Victor.

FROM A POSTCARD TO HIS SISTER

I t was nothing but up, pushing the bikes, eyes down to keep the wheels out of the worst ruts. Ray led and was around the turn, while I put distance between us to let the red dust broadcast, then tried a song: "Bike, bike, bike, to the best of thy speed, O Wheel." My Uncle Miles taught me the ditty when I was small and used to perch on his old 'ordinary' bicycle with its giant fore wheel. The words had to be crammed to fit the tune of "Down in a Coal Mine." Choking on dust, I stopped to pull the bandanna up over my nose and mouth. A family of quail, the babies almost as grown as their folks, scurried across the road in front of me.

At an outside hairpin, Ray was stopped. "Downhill from here," he yelled. "What's the cyclometer?" Pulling up, I rubbed the Veeder box clean. "Two hundred eighty-eight."

A lively stream cut a white and silver path through the canyon below, and Ray said, "Squaw River," as he drew from a bag the rope he'd picked up at the miner's shack. Holding the two ends, he measured to the middle.

"I know," I said. "We use the rope to hang ourselves, 'cause hanging's more honorable than not getting to the fair in time." He plopped in the dirt, laughing. I did too, mostly because I liked to make him laugh, also because he looked pretty funny sitting in that mess of rope dusted goggles to shoe-tops in rouge-colored dirt, his pants leg cut away like a big bite from a cookie.

When we'd sobered, he flicked open his pocketknife and sawed at the rope, cutting it into two equal lengths about four yards each. "Downhill we tie trees on behind. Save the brakes."

Ray sometimes had surprising ideas, though it was for me to approve, of course. "I'll chop the saplings," I allowed and dug in the bag for the hatchet. Off down the hillside, I hollered over my shoulder, "You tie the lengths to the back frames, those welds should hold," so he'd know who was in charge.

Later, with six-foot firs tied behind the bikes and looking like Paul Bunyan's feather dusters, we took off jerkily down the steep grade. I aimed between the ruts, bouncing over rocks, in and out of holes, all the time yanked at from behind. Steering was a tussle, but the savings on our New Departures would pay dividends. Ray kept two or three turns behind. Even so, he'd eat the dust that plumed in my wake. The distant breath of a train shushed louder, fainter, as it followed the ins and outs of a far-off canyon.

At the bottom under pine shade, we untied the trees and dragged them off the road near the bank of a stream. Across a wooden bridge a good thirty feet above water gabbling between hedges of maidenhair fern, my wheels glided over the boards and spaces as on butter. No thick dust, no tree yanking back. On the north side we left the bikes to scramble down to the water and fill our canteens. Hunkered there, we came alert at the loud squawk of a grouse or chicken in wild commotion. Across the stream and above the road we'd just come down, a small rough house was cozied among fruit trees, its roof smothered with cut fruit set out to dry on cheesecloth laid with aisles between for easy turning of the pieces. In the yard a near-grown boy, hatchet raised, held a flapping, screeching chicken on a tree-stump. He took a fresh grab of the chicken and came down hard, then tugged off the head and threw it to the flock, the poor chicken body still beating its wings, feathers flying.

Back on the road Ray loosed the lengths of rope from where we'd tied them on his handle bars. "These could help on the upgrade."

In a way I hoped his next rope trick wouldn't work, at least not as well as the last. He wound a length several times about the middle of his handlebars, took a couple more turns out to the grips, then left a yard or better to drop free from either handle. He tossed the second length to me and raised his smug eyebrows. "A horse takes a wagon up a hill, and you turn him left or right with the reins."

I grunted and harnessed up my bike. A rope end in each hand, he righted his bike and pushed from behind. Ropes guided the handlebars without his having to walk at the side. For all his religion and his book-reading, and his not liking track or basketball, some of his ideas would pass.

We stopped only once on the upgrade, to pull clear pitch from the trunk of a yellow pine. Chewing the tingly-bitter turpentine seemed to flavor the dust that filtered through my bandanna. At the summit the sun slanted low on the saplings as we cut them for the downgrade to the McCloud River, and by the time we tied them on, the sun was only a red fringe over a west hill.

We were most of the way down when we stopped at an outside turn and looked to the canyon bottom. There the river broadened to a wide dusky pool

Victor McDaniel on the McCloud River, with fish pens in the background.

almost directly below us. Along the far side, a necklace of campfires just now danced to life while knots of men talked and ambled about.

"Indians working the hatchery," Ray said, as though he expected to see exactly what we saw.

Down there a dog barked, and another, followed by a rough chorus of yips and yowls. Through the warm near-dark men's voices lofted up in unfamiliar highs and lows. Almost whispering, I said, "Think we should make camp near here? Indians might be curious if we get too close."

"Good idea," he agreed. Mounting, we rode without talk, even slowing with the brakes to reduce the dust from our saplings.

From an outlook flat enough to sleep on we squatted to look over. Fires were still sixty or seventy feet below. Fifteen or so men moved in slow shadows from one fire to the next, their strange talk rising, falling, merging with the murmur of the water.

First to roll up, Ray faced the road. His shoes and their valuable contents of watch and billiken covered over with his shirt were his pillow. I tied the laces of my shoes one to the other and tossed them toward his feet where they'd serve me the same. Back to back, we could see out both directions.

Working my ear into the comfort of a foot-hole, I locked my eyes on the dark that was the other side of the canyon. Its blackness wavered lesser, denser, the eerie campfire glows like feeble candles in a room too large. Men's voices also rose and sank and were made of sounds I'd never heard.

A dozen nights ago when I was a boy, all this might have kept me awake.

10

❧ ❧ ❧

8 o'clock the seining began. A large seine was run out by
workmen in boats and this was drawn in by a donkey engine.
It was a sight not to be forgotten to see the fight that followed.

FROM THEIR LETTER TO THE *SANTA ROSA PRESS DEMOCRAT*

S un bathed the other side of the canyon and now touched our
landing and the white, glossy bib of a gray squirrel about
three feet away, one front foot drooped slack, the rest of him
at keen attention. He watched me open the other eye.

"Hear that?" Ray sat up. The squirrel skittered down the bank.
"They've started work in the river." He was on his feet and rolling
his blanket as I laced up my second shoe.

No waves of talk from below this morning, only one deep, strong
voice calling something that sounded like "Haht, haht." Still in the
shade, men walked to and from a rectangular building upriver. In
the water almost directly below us, two rowboats maneuvered. A
man in each ran out a seine. Standing, he used an oar as pole as well
as paddle to position his boat, then bent over the side and adjusted
the net in the water. On the bank, four men stretched another seine
in the sun. Except for the boatmen's now and then "Haht," there
seemed no talk.

"Let's watch the haul," Ray yelled and lit out.

"Be something to write Finley about," I hollered from a couple
of lengths back.

"Donkey engine," Ray yelled, and I heard the ker-CHUNK,
huff-ker-CHUNK of piston action.

Across the river now, one end of the net was winding around a
large drum next to the boiler and engine; the other was tied about a
cottonwood some yards down shore. Engine strength would drag
the weight of the purse close in.

We dismounted on the corduroy bridge, as a dozen or so Indian
men rounded the corner of the building, rubber waders over their
trousers, shirtsleeves rolled above their underwear. Most sported

battered derby hats. They crossed the road ahead of us, walking without talk down the stream bank toward the pounding engine and the net. They seemed unaware of us on the bridge just a few yards away.

Under my breath, I said, "These really the same guys we heard loud-talking last night?"

We propped the bikes against the bridge rail and ran to the downriver side. Water fifteen or so feet below was dense with fish. Layer on layer of salmon, orange, red, yellow, brown and shades between, swam against the current. Some floated on the surface, their journey ended. "You could walk across on their bodies," I breathed.

Log enclosures jutted into the water from the bridge on the downstream side, four corrals about eight feet square and apparently lined with mesh. Inside them the fish were packed closer even than those on the outside, but each one pointed itself against the current, into the wall of the cage.

Downstream about two hundred feet away the four men who had stretched the seine on the bank were now hip deep in the water on the river side of the net. Scoop nets in hand, men waded to the center of the purse and fanned out, squaring themselves for footing. At a given instant, the men in the purse swung their nets up out of the water to hurl a fish, or two, three, into one of the skiffs alongside.

"Let's get closer." Ray grabbed his bike and pushed across the logs of the bridge, with me following. We leaned the bikes at the end of the pier and jumped to a boulder, onto another and down to run fast as the beach rocks allowed until, out of breath and ogle-eyed, we stood next to the boiler.

Men in the boats examined each fish when it slammed in. Some they tossed in piles at the bow ends. Rejects they heaved back in the river. The skiffs were sluggish to bring about, riding low in the bows under their loads of flopping fish, but the fellows poled until their boats headed upstream toward the traps.

A net man turned toward us and barked, "Sussinny."

I spun around, bumped into Ray and croaked, "C'mon!"

"Sussinny!" the man boomed louder.

Ray didn't budge, too busy looking back at the engine, and at a boy about ten, his hand on a ratchet, dark eyes fixed on us from out of his moon-shaped face, small under a derby too large. He wore man's clothing that would take a few more years to fill. Wide suspenders loosely held up a volume of trousers torn away at the

Indians seine fishing at the Government Fish Hatchery on the McCloud River.

bottom, leaving off in a raggedy line somewhere between calf and ankle.

"SUSS. . . !"

The boy pulled the ratchet. The drum spun free, rope paying out, the cylinder squealing with every revolution. The gruff fellow, along with several others, tugged the net out twenty feet or so to waist deep. Holding the seine, they watched the boatmen cache their cargoes into the log corrals, fish by battling fish.

When I looked around again, the boy was studying us. I nodded and sauntered off around the boiler, then stopped. Tonight at their campfires when the loud talk began, it would never do for the kid to report we were unfriendly. So I turned. "You work here?" He looked away to watch the fellows now waiting for the boatmen to row back to the net.

Beside me, Ray was fixed on the playing out of new skills right before our eyes.

Could have been this newness or maybe the unusual-sounding words of these folks, but together they made a certain discomfort in me. I wished we'd left the bikes against the pier on this side where we could see them.

"Father, brother, me, work here." I'd almost forgot my question.

Ray moved closer to hear him, as the boy told us he was McCloud and this was the government's hatchery. "Fish with no eggs, back to the river," he said. "Only milkers in traps. Long time ago all fish belong to McClouds, not government." His small arm, undershirt to his thumb joint, swept wide, suggesting the whole river. The boy tilted his head back to peer at us from under his grimed hat, his eyes of the softest black. Looking into them planted in me a new discomfort, a queer sort of guilt.

"Now government feed us. Men grow weak." His fawn's eyes darted upriver and back to us. Then his voice fell to less than the lap of the water, and we leaned to hear him. "Salmon." And he told us that the McClouds ate salmon in the night time because salmon made men strong. To make good babies and fight Modocs, he added and almost smiled.

With a wild swing the boy pretended to hit himself on the head, and down he fell. "Mo-doc." He groaned, jumped up and dashed along the bank past the stretched-out seine to bend over a plant. He picked a stalk and ate it down, blossom and all. "Kill enemy," he growled, then explained to us that saxifrage put in them much spirit to kill, and that soon their enemy Modocs would come back from the Oklahoma Reservation.

Then, as though startled, the lad looked to the river where the boatmen gathered the float edge of the net, held it in one hand and paddled with the other. In a rush the boy ran to the engine and fidgeted with the ratchet handle, his eyes never leaving the men in the water.

"Sussinny," Ray said, eager for more talk. "What's your name mean in your language?"

The youngster's eyes rested on the beach rocks at his feet. His brown toes curled around a pebble and let it fall, then with his foot he pointed to several thrush-like, stubby-tailed birds walking at the water's edge. Suddenly, quick as snow melts on a hot range, the birds disappeared into the water. Birds underwater?

The lad looked to where the birds had been. "Sussinny I am. Bird of good song." He jabbed a thumb to his chest. Then from low in his throat came a rolling sort of warble, the very sound I'd heard from birds near our camp on the Pit.

Then, the thunder-blast voice from the river, "Sussinny."

The boy whirled to the ratchet and pulled. Ray and I exchanged looks. I started up the beach. Ray was near wanting to stay, learn more about these people. A dragonfly whirred past my ear, its gauze-winged, blue-green sliver of a body doing right-angle turns.

Finally, tearing his gaze from the boy and the river, he followed. "Water ouzel. Sussinny's named for the water ouzel."

"And the kid might even come to be likable if we had the time. Which we don't. He going to follow us, you think?"

"No."

But neither of us turned to see. At the boulders we clambered up, then gave a boost to stand on the road. There my breath sucked in. The bikes! Flat in the dirt, they lay crazy-angled, canvas bags opened. Tablet paper was torn off and blown about. Sheets caught in the bridge logs. Air pump out of its clamp and tossed in the dirt. Fishing pole thrown to the side of the road. Matches dumped out of the jar and scattered. "No!" I yelped. The Pieper .22 was gone from Ray's bike, the wrap he was always careful to wind around it in a tangle behind a rock.

"Easy, Vic." He reached for my arm. "The bikes are still together."

I ran to them, rage exploding through me. "Had to see that fish haul. Oh yeah, had to light out of here like stuck muggies." I rummaged in a bag. "Hatchet still here."

"Revolver, rope here." Ray pulled his hand from a bag.

"Bike chain, lock, gone! Fish knife too!"

"Dried corn, the flitch of bacon, missing."

Nobody's life was in balance, but my fists clenched hard, and my stomach faced the other way about. If I could just land some blows into the scalawags that did this. I bleated, "They take the .22, bike chain, fish knife, but not the revolver or hatchet?"

Calm old Ray stuffed writing paper back down a bag. Didn't understand our losses could mean no Seattle, no fair. I shoved a hand down the blanket roll. Coin purse still there. My fingers searched. Frantic, I used both hands. "Billiken's gone!" I shouted.

"Easy, Vic."

"Our billiken's gone. Hear me?"

But he just picked up matches and jammed them in the jar. "Maybe fancied a doll, whoever it was."

Trying for control, I put the sandpaper and glue back in the repair kit. "Think it was Sussinny? Young enough he might want that little billiken."

"If it was him, I wager he watched us before we left the bikes. Sounded like he arrived late at that donkey engine."

I snapped the kit back on the frame. "Might not have been Sussinny. Could be those others have their special ways to run folks out of their country. Don't need to be Modocs, I expect. Every night down there eating their salmon and saxifrage, spoiling for fight."

Ray finished tying the fishing pole back to the frame. I kept an eye to the far edge of the road. "Haht, haht," came from the river. I breathed some easier and yanked down the straps on both bags. "Let's not play pokey around here, Ray."

Leaning his bike on the pier, he bent to pick up some tablet sheets pinned between the pier and a boulder. "You shove on. I'll be along." But he stayed crouched. "Hey, Vic!" I scrambled beside him. In the shade of a boulder lay two large salmon, as muddy-orange as any we'd seen, and damp-fresh. "Indians put aside their meals for the night, remember? Let's do turns about and take their fish." I reached for the closest tail. Ray aimed for the other. "I think these fish are here for us, Vic. I think it was Sussinny did all this. At the river he was eager to talk. In his way he felt like he already knew us. Could have stuck the paper here as a flag for us to find the salmon. Maybe a kind of game."

Hoisting the fish, I saw something dangling from its mouth. Two stalks of saxifrage, blossom ends out, had been threaded through to come out a gill.

"Sussinny all right," Ray chuckled. "Salmon and saxifrage. To make good babies and. . . " He interrupted himself, pointing to the mouth of his salmon. "Look!" Inside the fish's mouth, our billiken! He pulled it out and set the little figure on his palm.

"Welcome back, Jonah." He wiped the doll on his pants, then poked it down his pocket. I looked away. No cause to let Ray see I was pleased that foolish billiken was back on board.

Up the grade, steering with the ropes, listening to the "Haht, haht," I refocused. My eyes played sport with me. Everywhere I looked, in Ray's wheel tracks, under the pines, stubby-tailed sussinny birds darted along the water's edge and, quick as snow melts on a hot range, disappeared beneath the dust.

11

⬧⬧ ⬧⬧ ⬧⬧

During the afternoon we passed through country where
vegetation, trees, and everything had been killed by smelter
fumes.

FROM THEIR LETTER TO THE *SANTA ROSA PRESS DEMOCRAT*

We didn't stop till we reached the crest of the grade. Yanking
off our caps, we took a pull on our canteens. Ray said, "If
those Indians were tracking us, we'd know by now."

"If they want us to know, sure. If they don't. . . "

"Fish'll get mighty ripe on a day like this," he said, changing the
subject. "Should make camp early if we mean to eat 'em."

"That orange skin looks pretty foul to me." I wondered how he
could think to make an early camp with those Indians likely out
there waiting to ambush us for the gear they didn't take the first go-
around. My eyes riveted on a clump of deer brush that had jostled
in a curious way.

"Color doesn't put a bother in the Indians," he said, sounding of
a mind to eat the fish even if we had to heave 'em up later. "If we
lay over," Ray was saying. "Wait till the sun's past high, eat a fish,
the other might keep till dinner. Give me time to oil and clean the
bikes."

"So they catch us with our bikes in pieces, stuffing ourselves?" I
hopped on and stayed mounted, my temper rising with every jounce
down a rut. Besides, I roiled at losing the old fish knife Uncle Miles
gave me. Sussinny or somebody would use that knife to clean his
fish tonight. After the earthquake of aught six, when Papa and I
searched Santa Rosa wreckage for the dead and injured, we'd come
on poor Uncle Miles pinned under a girder beneath a jumble of dirt
and boards. "Get a gun, Cecil," he'd pleaded to Papa. But Papa
couldn't do it. Later we heard his good friend shot him, and Papa
forever worried he'd failed his brother. Now I'd failed him too; I'd
lost the grand knife he'd bought up in the Klondike in '98 and
given "to the finest boy in town," as he liked to say.

I jumped off to push up the next grade, Ray right behind me. Sweat dribbled from under my cap-band and dripped off my nose. Above the road the hill was scoured earth. Leafless, bleached-bone tree trunks studded putty-colored ridge humps, and wispy brush carcasses clung to sterile-looking dirt.

"Smelter kill," Ray said. "Copper in the Keswick country. Remember? Papers told about all the devastation." I grunted as though I remembered. I did remember Papa talking to his friend Jim Ramage about if California had somebody besides Gillette for governor, he'd likely see that the smelters aimed their corruption another way than the mountains to the north. Hills on both sides of us now were baked-out, dried-up, naked tree trunks lifeless as monuments in a graveyard. But, no brush, no trees meant no place to hide an Indian.

I got off to push over a rickety bridge across what should be, according to the map, Salt Creek. Here I yanked the fish out of my pack and gave it a mighty throw up the hillside.

Water below tumbled white and noisy around rocks and swirled into deep green pools that looked mighty inviting. "I'm going in," I hollered to Ray, now bumping over the bridge. My clothes in a pile, I bolted down the bank.

"Don't drink the water," he yelled, laying his bike by mine.

My breath back after the cold plunge, I shouted, "Throw out that fish. Smells clear down here."

I sloshed about, dunked my head, sputtered up to see Ray's clothes in a heap and him tugging the rotten salmon from his pack. He gave it a fine heave across the road, then lunged down the bank into the water. Of a sudden my hair yanked back. "Sorry, fella, thought that scalp was on a Modoc." And he churned off upstream. I plowed after him. "Modoc, huh!" We thrashed about, the water putting such a charge in us.

After a time, dressed and alive again, we pushed off up the hill. Old Shasta Mountain reared itself to total the whole north sky. Past a draw, pushing the bikes around holes the size of dishpans, the road narrowed to scant wagon width, the outside road edge having fallen away. "No growth to hold the ground," Ray yelled up, as though I couldn't figure that out.

So I said, "Five more miles and we rack three hundred. Make that four miles." Ray would have liked the Veeder box mounted on his bike, in spite of what he said about it making no difference to him. I smiled at the ping, ping of the metal finger on spokes that counted each sluggish wheel turn.

Stubbing on something in the dust, I winced and pulled back. In a flying kick I brought up a horseshoe and flung it over the side. The road was enough to make an animal cast a shoe, steep, narrow, the inside rut deeply troughed, gouged by mattocks of wagon drivers forging a lower track to keep their rigs level and serve as safety against tipping or rolling over the bank.

Stopped at the crest, Ray picked up porcupine quills and announced, "We'll soon see life." Right enough, down the canyon late light showed pines and manzanita, firs and oaks in alive-greens. In the canyon bottom the Sacramento River was a wiggly, shining thread. Then the air throbbed, more with vibration than sound, and a train's whistle shrilled. Chuff-huff, chuff-huff, the canyon repeated the snorting rhythm and the wail, layer on layer, till the beginning had no direction.

"Must have just come out of a tunnel," Ray said. About three quarters of a mile down canyon the train crossed the river on a trestle, smoke in a horizontal cone over the engine and tender, too little breeze to take it any place. Even up here the sun would soon drop. And as we dropped, Shasta Mountain's great white-orange eye did slowly close. Pines on either side of the road hummed to themselves, and the air smelled of hot grass and leaves and life. Our road crossed on a truss bridge just up from the trestle, and we made camp on the rocky beach of the shadowy river.

"Trout here are likely to bite on red flannel," Ray said, working at his fish line. How did he know these things? I busied myself dragging from the bank thick pine boughs to sleep on.

Later, trout in our bellies and us bedded down, the air smelled of pines and skunk and river. Over the drone of the water, I said, "Be no trouble to take the cyclometer off my bike. We could mount it on yours for the rest of the trip. What d'you say?" But he was already asleep, or maybe too far into prayer to answer.

❦

Next morning the sun crept slowly down the west side of the canyon as we ate our trout and sniffed wood smoke. It was only after Ray had buried the coals that he discovered we'd had a visitor in the night. "It's not here!" he yelled from behind the boulder where the bikes leaned.

"What's not there?"

"My pack! It's gone!" He was bent over, searching.

I was beside him. "Look!" I pointed near the water's edge where drag marks jagged a stretch of sand. Paw prints big as soup bowls led up river.

"Bear!" We said together.

We followed the tracks to a willow thicket about thirty yards from camp where, in a clump of grass, the pack lay flap open, toilet paper in a stringy wad half in, half out. Ray picked up the pack. "Straps, buckle okay. Just tears in the flap. And our pears mashed all to slime."

I sniffed. "Bear was likely peeved that foul smell had no fish to go with it." In no mood for joshing, Ray slung the pack over his shoulder.

The river here was forty or fifty feet wide, its deep green turned to yellow shimmer with the sun spilling on it. I picked up a small flat rock, curled a forefinger around it and skipped it down river. "Our friend, he could have been a grizzly."

"There's no guessing," Ray said, and we fell quiet as we were off up the bank and across the tracks.

"Travel the railroad?" I said. "No worse dust than the road. And no steep grades." A part of me figured a bear might be smart enough to stay clear of the tracks.

"Sure, see how it goes. We can always get back to the road."

I even mounted, but soon got off when thick brush blocked the path beside the tracks. Lodged in and under the growth were oddments thrown from trains: empty Lucky Strike and Boar's Head tobacco cans, a container box for Curtis Consumptive Cure where some poor devil maybe threw it on his way to Shasta Springs thinking he wouldn't be needing it any more. Above us, the cut of the wagon road wound in and out of the folds of the mountain. Below, the river glinted in full sun. Another bridge angled over the river ahead. "Cross with the rails? Or climb to the road?" I yelled back.

"Stick with the rails."

I pushed around a washout in the trail and wondered how we could ever tell folks in our letters just how deep these canyons really were, or how much sky that Shasta took up when she showed herself. Near the high bridge I laid down my bike and put an ear to the rail. No clicks, no hum, only smooth metal burning my skin. "No trains," I called. A few yards behind, Ray took no chances. Bottom up, he listened to the other rail.

"Let's go," I said, and pushed off, trying to swallow the fright that clutched my insides. I'd never liked heights. We walked between the rails across the narrow span, the bikes bumping at our sides. Between me and the far-below water, only the ties. My knees went soft, and I kept close watch on the ties two or three ahead, rather than the one I was about to step on. But nothing separated me from the slit after slit of moving water sixty or so feet straight down. My palms went icy sick. My head floated free. I stepped along smartly. If my eyes lingered on the water I could be pulled toward it. A quarter of the way across my breath came shallow and in little bursts. A breeze whistled through the bridge struts. Look at the boards ahead. Not through. Half way now, thump, bump. I gripped the handlebars, hanging on. Sweat poured from under my cap-band to drip in my eyes.

"Hey, wait up!" Ray called.

Racing the last few feet off the bridge, I aimed for a rock, stumbled and plopped, my bike sprawling.

"You okay?" Ray bumped over the last of the bridge ties.

"Fine," I lied, eyes down.

"Sure?" He stood in front of me.

"Sure." I looked up, but slowly.

Ray laid down his bike, dropped to his knees, and pressed an ear to the rail. Turning, I saw why. No more than a hundred feet ahead was the black mouth of a tunnel in the side of the steep hill. "No trains." He jumped up, grabbed his bike and was off. Half running to catch up, my legs gained starch. Sound conduction in rails was good for five or six miles, but there was no cause to loiter.

Inside, the tunnel was blacker than just dark, but gradually my eyes put a shape to objects and space. We walked between the rails because the metal picked up sheen, and because the tunnel was only wide enough on either side for a man, but not a bike with a broad load. My eyes accustomed now, I expected to see light at the other end, but none shone. Probably a bend in the tunnel, enough to keep the day on the other side. Sunlight from our entrance dimmed, gradually fading to a gauze of mostly how we remembered things, the sooted rock faces each side, the occasional iron rod and nut protruding from the tunnel's ceiling to bolt back rock falls.

"Can you see?" My voice came back to me like the halloos my sister Alma and I used to send down the well as we lay with our faces over the edge.

"Not a glimmer," Ray answered, sounding off in a hole.

I shivered. Would bears hide in tunnels, I wondered. But the cool was a relief, cool almost to dampness. I wished I'd put on my shirt. More, I wished we'd at least have taken time to light our lamps. But we should keep walking, past the bend, into light. Twang, twang, went the cyclometer finger.

Suddenly, an explosion! I missed a tie and stumbled before I realized Ray had sneezed. "Let's get out of here," I cried unnerved.

"We'll be out soon, Vic."

"See any light?"

"Not yet. This curve is a long one."

Air whooshed past my head. "Bats!" I yelled, and my shout came back from all directions. I threw an arm across my face. Stories of bats pecking out eyes shuddered through me. But as quick as they came, they were gone. Then wham on the bill of my cap! A splat! Another plop dumped on my ear, my shoulder, behind me, everywhere thunks of water. Walking faster, I shook all over as the damp air chilled my skin and clothes.

"Light ahead!" Ray hollered.

I craned left, right. "I don't see it." Then I saw. Maybe a quarter mile down tunnel, a disc of light. "It's there all right!" I sprinted after Ray bobbing black against the hole of daylight.

Then, a blast! From behind us a train whistle screamed through the rock tube, one long blow. Still a distance off, thank the Lord. I fumbled through what I knew of locomotive talk. One long, the approach warning. Was the train about to cross the bridge? Enter the tunnel? Against the growing light, Ray's bike silhouette bounced faster. We could make it! My bike pounded beside me.

Another blast! Wildly closer! Sustained! The whistle howled down the tunnel, skinned my ears. God, oh God, the train was about to come in here with us!

"Can't make it, Ray!" In a piece I jumped with my bike over the left rail onto the narrow shoulder and scrunched the wheels to the wall. The train's headlight blared at the black rock of the tunnel's bend. My saddlebags bulged too wide. I punched the bag, flattening whatever was inside. I fought the crossways blanket roll. Light was broad white, filling the tunnel. The roar of the engine slammed into my bones, pained my ears.

Where was Ray? Scrambling in front of my bike, I loosed the belt on the roll. There he was! Ahead, mashed to the wall, watching me. The belt fell. I tugged the blanket off, turned it parallel. Bright light beaconed the charred walls. Noise exploded in my head. Huge, black, the engine steamed around the bend, close, gigantic. But I had to get around the bike, to the end nearest the train. Or be carried along if the bike hung up. The iron beast boomed down. I dashed toward the giant snout, around the bike, and spread-eagled against the rock as the cowcatcher fanned wide-toothed in front of me, its outside edge just missing my shoes.

Smoke thick as cotton singed my nose, throat. I coughed, my eyes following the cowcatcher past my bulging saddlebag. The grate-like apron sped on. The deafening colossus, scant inches from me, charged by.

Ray. Would he think to stand toward the train from his bike? Choking, my eyes hot pokers, tears spurting, I was helpless, frozen against the rock wall. The engine's lead wheels rumbled before me, the steam cylinder massive. I blinked and gasped. A jag of rock was a knife between my shoulders. The drive rod thrust around, over, close to my kneecaps, the noise bursting my head. God, You better take care of Your Ray, because I can't. A drive wheel rumbled past, and another, screeching, pounding, and a third. The firebox walled by, its small side door open to angry orange flames. Below, coals glowed eerie bright in the ash catcher. I hacked, tears squirting. Now the engine's trailing wheel.

"Hey! You!" a voice bawled. It was the fireman, his head out the cab up there, his face bald terror. He was by me then and looking back. Nothing he could do. Now he would be telling the engineer.

I squeezed my eyes shut. Wheels passed. And passed. Cars rattled and squeaked close to my head, as the engine's thunder faded outside the tunnel. I couldn't open my eyes for the sting, but I imagined the expressions of the people inside to see through their closed windows a blackened clown only a hand grab away. More wheels clicked by. Then, hollow clanking, and the last car. Slowly I unsqueezed my eyes. The final wheels jangled past. Peeling from the wall, I coughed, doubled over. Smoke fogged blue against the light, a halo around the clacketing train.

There he was! A ball in the dirt. But moving. Not dead, thank God. On his hands and knees, Ray crawled slowly. I scrambled over the tracks, tripped but didn't go down. He wasn't tangled in the bicycle, but the train could have mauled him. God, please help us!

Several yards from him yet, I heard a train's whistle. One long, three short. Another train? I dropped by Ray.

"You there!" A voice cannoned from the direction of the train.

Ray left off crawling. Raising his head, he sat on his heels. The man ran toward us now from the last car that had stopped just outside the tunnel.

"You hurt?" he called.

"Don't know," I shouted back. Ray's face was black with soot, but no blood showed.

The big man ground gravel as he stopped. "You got no business in this tunnel! No business!" He puffed, out of breath. "You fellows hurt?"

"I don't think so, sir." I stood up. Ray did too, thank the Lord.

"You realize you could get bad hurt fooling around in a tunnel like this? Killed even?" We nodded.

"You stopped that train out there. You know that? All those people going to be late because a couple galoots want to play hide and seek in a tunnel." He glared at us. "Southern Pacific could turn the law on you, you know that?"

"We do, sir," I said.

"We'll travel the roads from now on, sir." Ray used his minister's voice.

The fellow's big shoulders slacked a little, and he swiveled his gaze to the blackened wall. "Well, for—" He spied Ray's wheel. The man shook his head, gravel crunching under his heel as he turned to go. "Bicycles!" he sputtered, then stopped. Bending down, he picked something up and held it in his hand. Hardly turning, he tossed it to us. "Here. For good luck."

Ray caught it. "Thank you, sir." His smile broke white over his sooted face and he held up the billiken. "Been combing the dirt looking for it. Never thought it could pop that far up the track."

12

❀   ❀   ❀

Started out for Dunsmuir. Found good roads, most were down hill. At Dunsmuir we saw the round house and many things of interest, one of which was a large snow plough.

FROM THEIR LETTER TO THE *SANTA ROSA PRESS DEMOCRAT*

That night, after we'd soaped ourselves and our clothes in the river, I hung the duds on bushes near the fire. Camp was under the uphill footings of the railroad bridge we'd just crossed—I hoped it was my last—to put us back on the road side of the river. Our fire crackled in the hobo pit, a blackened circle of rocks complete with the usual just-as-blackened Folger's Golden Gate coffee can.

"Remember the tramp used to come through Santa Rosa? Called himself 'A-Number-One-Hobo?' " I asked.

On his knees in front of the fire, Ray flipped the fish he held between sticks. "Sure. Always figured to get a handout from Luther Burbank. Paid for it by carving an Indian head out of one of Burbank's potatoes." He chuckled.

Only the top of the canyon was still light by the time we laid the fattest pine bough we could find crossways for the head of our bed. Poking the butt ends of the other branches under it, we took care the fullness and curve of them bowed upward, giving us a fine mattress over two feet thick.

Next morning, after replenishing the wood stack, true to hobo tradition, we stood looking at the steep hillside and the cut of the road a good quarter mile up.

"It'll be some scrabble through all that brush and rock," I said, grabbing my wheel fore and aft.

"No other way to get there." Ray lifted his bike over a manzanita.

Over and around boulders big as wagons, through tangles of thorny brush that dug into the canvas bags, sliding on loose shale, we bucked and butted our wheels up the hill on a pitch steep as a wall. At last I lifted my bike over the fill boulders. One last heave and I plunked it in good old road dirt. "Yee-iiiii!" I shot my fists in the air.

Behind me Ray grinned in a face scratched and bleeding, then grunted his wheel onto the road.

"You're enough to sour milk," I welcomed him.

"And I doubt Mrs. Astor would be inviting you to tea."

"Cyclometer's at 310," I announced, setting out. Ruts were shallow, the grade slight, and the surface hard-packed. A day to clock miles. Morning was well on when we stopped under Castle Crags, the huge slab-sided, slate-colored rocks high above the road. Aglow in early-sun orange, the rocks up there put a kind of worship in me, and I stopped chomping my carrot. His eyes fixed on the big rocks too, Ray must have felt my thoughts. "Today's Sunday, Vic," he said softly.

A short incline dropped us into the little town of Castella where dressed-up folks nodded as we pedaled by. One little girl following after her papa reminded me of Snook, Hazel, my little sister. We called her Snook after Snookums in the funnies.

The road skimmed behind us as if we were cream on a milk pan. There'd be a Seattle for us sure. Yes sir, we'd see Roltair's Original House Upside Down, where everybody looked as if he were standing on his head. And the Joy Wheel. What a ride that must be, and I leaned back in the saddle, stuck my legs straight out and let the air rush up my trouser legs. But a chuckhole sat me straight, an onion shooting from my hand to bounce off the side of the road. I kept my seat now and watched down canyon for Dunsmuir to show itself.

Then around a bend, tin-roofed houses climbed the hill like so many cleated stairs, and we were riding up the main street of Dunsmuir. Past the closed doors of a harness shop, I thought how those doors would be open on any other day of the week. Inside, saddlers would punch out holes with their awls and run thread across the rosin held in their palms, just like old Belden and Heir in Santa Rosa.

"Watch out!" Ray yelled, and I dodged a dung flop.

Now he coasted, his ear cocked. "Hear that?" Swiveling, I saw smoke feather up from behind the buildings that separated us from the tracks. An engine bell tolled, rich and deep. Air hissed from brakes as a train slowed to a stop.

"Freight. Too many cars for a passenger," I said importantly.

Ray nodded. "Dunsmuir's a division point. Want to take a look at the roundhouse?"

"You bet." I leaned to turn toward the chunk-chunk of rail cars stopping. "Maybe watch 'em add another engine for the pull up the mountains."

At the tracks we crossed in front of the wheezing engine. Not the one we'd met up with in the tunnel. Even so, my legs took on a respect and stepped right along till we gained the other side, out of the path of that cowcatcher.

"G'day." A fireman smiled down at us from the tender where he stood holding a rope. He pulled it, and a spout from the water tower alongside groaned, tipped out, and a wide stream gushed from it into the tank of the tender. The engine was a 4-6-2: four leading wheels, six driving wheels, two trailing.

Off to the left a rail yard spread larger, busier than any I'd ever seen. More tracks laid here in one place, more switches and frog spurs than a soul might conjure. Yard men everywhere. They greased, banged on, hammered at, and climbed over the cars. And all this commotion on a Sunday. The roundhouse was at the far side. From here its stalls looked to number more than a dozen, with a good half occupied.

"Watch yourself!" Ray grabbed my arm, as my bike rammed hard. In front of me a young man sprawled on the tie stubs. Scrambling to his knees, he grabbed for an oilcan and wiping rag near the car's axle box.

"Sorry," I apologized.

The fellow stood up to short, bandy-legged height and grinned from under his floppy hat. "No harm. Around here, I never thought to get toppled by a bicycle."

"I'm sorry," I said again. "Looking every place but where I was going."

"You fellas aim to look, you best park them wheels. Yard bulls is gettin' mighty pinch-nosed about train tramps. With those packs they'll pin you for freight-hoppers sure."

"Yard bulls?" Ray looked puzzled.

"Railroad police," I said, too loud, over the clank of cars being coupled on the next track. "Thanks," I said to the oiler, down in a squat again. He wiped his rag over the axle and flicked a glob into the can. "Want a good ride to Portland? Nice and cool. Just climb in this here refrigeration car." He gestured at the wide sliding door above him, then plugged the oil spout to another hole. "'Bout half loaded. Best kind of ride. Not much bounce."

I looked at Ray. He wrinkled his forehead, as though he thought I was tempted. "Thanks anyway," he told him. "These wheels do us fine."

We pushed on toward the roundhouse, the thump of our tires on the ties almost in rhythm to heavy hammering the other side of the car. Two cars later, alongside a flatcar of piled lumber, heavy footfalls pounded behind us. I looked around. A red-faced fellow, legs pumping hard toward us, shouted, "That's them!"

"You see 'em unload?" somebody yelled.

"Hey, you two. You're under arrest!"

My wheel bounced high as I ran. Off to the right Ray crossed a set of tracks, and another, his bike flying beside him. I doubled around two coupled cars.

"Just kids," the first one yelled.

"Men," hollered the other. "Hey, stiffs! You're under arrest!"

I caught up with Ray. We crossed tracks just ahead of the wheels of an empty flatcar. "We'll have to give up," I panted.

"Next tracks, Vic! See that plow?" He lifted his bike and plunked it the other side of a rail, with no lost stride. I looked behind us. Under a gondola car four pant legs churned. We ran forward of the mammoth engine along the length of one of the snowplow's high fixed-blade sides. At its front end we lifted the bikes over a crosspiece. Inside the plow was space for me next to one blade, Ray next to the other, just ahead of the huge rotary core.

Flat against the metal, we stood with our bikes leaning into us. The men's agitated voices carried above the yard noise but sounded a distance away.

"Sunday's near to over," Ray whispered. "And me just getting around to pray."

I smiled. "I might add my own this time."

The bulls yelled back and forth, closer, still bothered. Ray's words were muffled as he talked to his God, ". . . for Vic . . . safely . . . ."

"Dumb, pimply-faced bastards! Lookin' for a free ride," snarled close to the plow. Ray and I locked eyes, still as moles in a graveyard. Gravel crunched and stopped. "Dirty loafers. I'd like to—" An engine huffed, eating the threat.

When the breath went out of the locomotive, we held ours and listened. Seconds, minutes, two, three. No gravel gritted, no words rasped. Another minute, and Ray nodded. Gingerly he inched his bike from where it leaned against him. "Br-r-ring!" His bell cut through the air, freezing us rigid. In a short bit Ray lifted his bike toward the crosspiece. "Not yet!" I mouthed, gesturing like a wild man. He stopped, craned around the end of the blade, then nodded and lifted the bike up and over.

My heart banged against my teeth. We could be walking straight into handcuffs or a billy club. But I lifted my old Sears Acme quiet as could be and hoisted it over the crosspiece. Once outside I looked about, then peered under the plow for trouser legs on the other side. Ray shoved off, half carrying his bike. I followed, doing the same. We set out north between two flatcars loaded with milled lumber that smelled of pine. Scanning right, left, I ran and rehearsed. At the slightest movement I'd drop the bike and be all over them before they could blackjack us. I hoped Ray would think to do the same. But the only motion was a cigarette paper scuttling over the gravel in the small breeze. The only sounds were the hiss of air brakes, a worker shouting, a far-off whistle and a now and again bang on metal.

Two yard hands, likely goldbricking, lounged toward us.

"G'day," they mumbled as we ran by.

At the yard's boundary Ray looked up canyon. "Follow the main north tracks?"

"Sure. We'll find the wagon road later."

At last able to mount, we rode the level path to the side of the tracks, ears buttoned back, tuned to a bull's roar. Once we'd rounded a bend, I slowed and dared a look behind us. No bulls, no rail yard. Only jags of rock on the canyon side and the Sacramento roiling green and white not far below.

13

❀ ❀ ❀

Dear Mama, Arrived at Shasta Springs. Right among 'em here.
City sports. Drank so much glacier water could hardly come
down these bridges. Only fourteen miles from Mt. Shasta. I tell
you it's a big lump of dirt all right. Will send you a picture of it from
Sisson. Please send me about fifty cents for cards if you can
spare it, Mama? Send P.O. order when I let you know where I'll
be. Victor.

FROM A PICTURE POSTCARD HOME

The wagon road to Shasta Springs was straight up. Ahead, Ray slogged in a cloud of dust. I tasted the grit of my own cloud, and my eyes burned. Dog-belly deep the fine silt felt like pillow down. Big as God, Shasta Mountain, dazzling in late-afternoon golds, blocked the sky. But here in the canyon, twilight lowered fast. Blurred shadows deceived the trees, even the turns of the road. Then, just past a wide bend we saw the glow of lights: buildings of the resort.

I pulled up to where Ray stopped and said, "Bed down here by the road? Easier to pack up and be gone at first light, before the swells pick up our scent on their way to the ozone springs."

"For sure we don't want to get any closer."

Without making a fire, we ate the last of our vegetables and rolled up next to the road where we could get away quick and early.

Daybreak showed we were nearer the big hotel than we'd thought and we scurried to pack ourselves up and be gone. By the time we found the path to the handrail bridges down the hill to the springs the skyful of mountain was ablaze in early morning pink.

Back and forth and back and forth the bridges zigzagged across the narrow ravine of ferns and thick growth that carried the booming, cascading water. On a landing about halfway to the bottom we left our wheels by a small, deep pool. Then, dropping to our bellies, faces in the icy water, we drank. Farther down the path several springs seeped from the bank, and at the bottom near the train depot the famous mineral and ozone springs sported lettered signs and board steps to stand on while you drank. We drank so we could say we had, but the water tasted curative and smelled faintly like Mama's spring tonic.

Hearing voices from high on the path, we chased back up the ravine to where we'd left the bikes. Four young ladies came strolling down, holding hands two by two and laughing. Dressed in soft white waists and skirts that rippled, they quieted as we pushed by them, moving aside for us more than they needed. I wished Ray and I had taken time to wash ourselves free of dirt.

Back on the road dust was too deep to stay mounted. I hollered up to Ray, "What's that water stuff they're selling at the fair?"

" 'Zarembo,' " he shouted back as he pushed up the grade. " 'Water from under the Sea.' "

"Now what's the sense of that?"

The silliness of such an idea and Ray's not bothering an answer added to my irritation at the dust, now ten, maybe eleven inches deep. Pushing, wading through it was like shoving through cotton batting. "About five weeks till October first," I yelled, giving it the sound of a reprimand as I wiped a hand over the cyclometer. "Three hundred fifty-six miles to here."

Ray was stopped ahead. Again no answer, as he pointed to a fallen log by the side of the road, its bark shredded and peeled. "Claw marks. Bears."

"Bears!" I hollered. His calm heaped onto my stack of irritations, I plowed on past. "Now bears!" I yelled back. "A third of our time gone. Three times two is six weeks, not five. We're near out of money. A dollar seventy-four cents left. And now bears."

"We'll make it, Vic," he said, catching up. "Best we work a few days at Weed. Come Oregon we'll do better on roads. Make up for lost days."

"Just what do you know of Oregon roads?"

It was eight full hours after we left Shasta Springs that we pulled in to Sisson only six miles away. At its first horse trough Ray splashed water over his hair and face and arms while I braced a knee against the wide corner of the trough and dried off with a clean shirt. The town sat smack on the haunches of the great Shasta like a cub on its mama. But the little place had a hurry about it; covered carts and wagons and people rattled and talked along the dusty main

POST CARD

This space for writing

This side is for the Address

Mr. O. H. McDaniel

653 Sonoma Ave.

Santa Rosa,

Cal.

Mt. Shasta from Sisson, California

street. On the sidewalk beside us two boys in bib overalls and short-billed caps stopped to ogle our bikes. The smaller fellow reached out to touch Ray's blanket roll.

Ray wiped his bandanna over his hair and face. "You boys want to give this bell a good stout ring?" The taller boy let the little fellow go first. His small hand on the dome partly covered the serpent design while with the other he leaned into the lever. The ring of it made both boys' eyes sprout. The older boy had his turn then, and we were off.

Outside town to the north a giant cinder cone rose straight up from the valley floor, a thrust of black boulders maybe a thousand feet high. Dust here was only an inch or two, so we stayed mounted on the shallow-rutted road. Nearer the cone, I saw its blackness came from the millions of shadows cast by small rock faces. Struck by the late sun the whole mass was tinged dark lavender, the deep color echoing in the scatter of firs that somehow found a toe grip on the cone's sheer walls. To the right of her black upstart, snowy mother mountain was a proud orange in the last light.

Air rushing cool past my ears and tingling my face put a smile in me. Made me remember a good smile I had in fourth grade when Mr. Mallory lent Papa six hundred dollars for lumber to build the house on Sonoma Avenue. The money was all in twenty-dollar double eagles. Mama and Papa, Alma, Olive and I stacked them in rows on the kitchen table. And we all smiled. Poor little Snooks, we couldn't let her at them for fear she might hide a piece or two to play with. Just around the butte, a strong north wind hit us, slowing our pace, and I stood on the pedals. All of a sudden sand layered the road, deep in places, and the wind was a cold gale.

"Bed down?" I hollered up.

He slowed for me. "Let's make town. Look for work in the morning."

"Can't manage this sand after dark anyway." Then, rounding a bend, I pointed. "Look!" Halfway up the south face of what the map said was Mt. Eddy raged a full-blown forest fire. We stopped, fascinated.

Ray said, "Think we should go fight the fire?"

"Wind takes it close to town we'll have no choice, along with everybody else. For now let's bed down." Around the next curve in the road another fire glow came to view, a lumber yard's cone-shaped sawdust burner. I clapped a hand on Ray's shoulder. "There's our work."

Just before the town of Weed we rolled up in a field. It was long past dusk, but the great white mountain had captured part of the day and watched us with an alien light. Sometime in the night the wind changed, and I woke up cold. Rolling tighter, I backed closer to Ray. The sky over the fire had reddened, pulsing ripe near the horizon. From the woods across the field an owl screeched long and frantic. I hoped Ray hadn't forgotten to pray.

14

⚜ ⚜ ⚜

From Victor McDaniel and Ray Francisco, the *Press Democrat*'s Seattle Exposition Bicycle Team, two interesting letters have come to hand. The boys have been having a hard time of it getting over mountain grades and have had their share of troubles, as will be seen from perusal of their letters: "We had such a hard job pushing our wheels from Sisson to Weed through the sand and dust that we concluded to stay a while in Weed."

THE *SANTA ROSA PRESS DEMOCRAT*

*T*wo dollars a day and it's over there you vould load hup." The foreman of the sash and door factory was a big man, a blond, square-faced Scandinavian. He gestured to the right of the barn-sized opening of the long, tin-roofed building. There baled, wired-together box shooks, end tabs, sides, bottoms for the making of boxes, were stacked in long rows.

The three of us stood facing outside to a rail spur. An empty car waited gape-doored. In the distance, mountains lay blue and vague behind a pall of smoke. During the night the wind had turned about and would soon strangle the fire. Or so we'd been told by the fruit farmer we met on the road this morning.

"We'd like to work the week out, sir," Ray shouted over the whines of saws behind us. The foreman nodded and led off toward the end of the work arena, with us falling in behind.

On the far side of the building a saw droned. We filed by a sweating workman feeding milled slabs to a saw that screeched as it bit in, and on past two helpers about our age shoving a dolly with a huge bin on it. Never straightening, they picked up scrap and tossed bits and pieces into the bin. The hot, noisy air was sweet with pine. Following the foreman's broad-striped overalls, I blinked at a sudden storm of sawdust while saws screamed around us. Two dollars a day. These bicycle bums had landed on the sunny side of the hedge this day.

At the end of the building the foreman pointed at two hand trucks leaning against the wall. "You men good and strong. Load the shook fast and that car been filled in nothing time. But—" A saw squealed. "You got to watch out you don't snag the vire holds 'em bundled together. Shooks scatter like hens from the coop. Keep those piles apart. Ends, sides, bottoms, bottoms got no knots, so to take the veight from the fruit." He slapped me on the back. "Other boys vill show you the grub house comes twelve o'clock." And he strode off.

We grabbed the hand trucks and began loading. When I'd hoisted up the last bale of side slats, I shoved a foot at the under bar and kicked the wheels ahead. Behind us, saws buzzed, machinery clanked. At the heavy metal plate that bridged platform to rail car floor, I balanced the truck while Ray loaded inside the car. A glance at our bicycles against the side of the building told me they were where we'd left them, wheels interlocked, duffel, frame, all a uniform dirt color.

Ray clattered his empty truck out of the car and back across the ramp to set off for his next load. Inside the car I eased the truck from under the stack and put a hand on it to be sure it steadied. This shook could wind up crating Sebastopol gravensteins, and I thought of those old box-makers in the fruit sheds back home. For as long as they allowed, I'd watch them, hands flying, flipping their box-maker's hatchet to pound with its griddle end a nail at a time out of the storage between thumb and forefinger.

I was rattling the empty truck back across the ramp when a whistle shrilled. In the building saws groaned to a stop, motors rumbled and quieted. Men straightened, smiling, talking, pulled tobacco from their pockets. Ray and I parked the hand trucks and followed the migration.

Inside the long grub house we hung our hats with the rest on pegs along the wall, then queued up at the end of the line. A long-faced man handed out tin plates and cups. The line moved on to a large Chinese fellow who dug a dipper into an iron vat and plopped stew on the plates like cow splats in a bucket. We sat in the middle of one of the long tables. Men around us ate like it was the reason for the day. One already stepped over the bench to go through the line again.

"Boy!" A rough-looking man at the end of our table called across the room to a frail lad standing behind the men and pouring water in their cups from a great graniteware pitcher. The boy aimed for our table, his gait uneven, one leg sadly shorter than the other. He filled the cup of the rough-looking fellow, then looked up for others. His eyes were a startled blue under his lank blond hair. "Boy!" hollered a fellow at the table next to ours. The lad limped to him.

"Go back for more?" I asked Ray. He shook his head, pulled out his watch and swung a leg over the bench, "We've just got time to wheel to town. Get a chain and lock for the bikes."

"What about money?"

"We have a dollar six bits and making more. Can't leave the bikes without chaining."

It was a quick ride to the general store where we found a sturdy chain and lock for a dollar four bits, and were back, the bikes secured through both rear wheels, before the last straggle of workers shambled down from the grub house. The whistle blasted twice. Without looking to hurry, the men were at their stations almost before the whistle quit the second time, cranking up machinery, tugging at pieces of lumber.

After work and supper, our bellies bulging with macaroni and cheese and bread pudding with raisins, we decided we best roll up near our gear. The bunkhouse would have been a more sociable place but, after pumping air in Ray's almost flat tire, we wheeled off to the same field, built a fire and settled close to it.

"Uncommon, wasn't it," I said, watching Ray whittle on a stick. "How Sussinny feared the Modocs coming back."

Ray looked up. "Always been enemies. McClouds knew old Taft was returning Modocs to their Oregon-California homelands. McClouds, Pits, all the Wintun peoples, they'd know about the trouble back on the Oklahoma Reservation. Might figure Modocs would bring the trouble back with 'em."

My eyes fastened on the upper third of the big mountain, still several shades whiter than lower down. "Those Snakes are giving the government plenty of worry," I said. "Taft probably decided a few less Indians of one kind or another might make things more peaceable back there." I couldn't be sure if I'd seen a movement, slow and stealthy, across the field.

Ray threw his whittling stick in the fire. It brightened where the pitch bubbled. "Modocs aren't being returned to land through here though. On the reservation in Oregon they'll just be near their own country, not in it."

The stick burned evenly now. Dark had closed in, but the mountain up there seemed to give off a brightness. Our faces hot, backs cold, we pulled the fire apart. Coals glowed in a heap off to the side, and we hurried to roll up while the ground was still warm. After a time I said, "You believe those stories about how the Chinese smuggle girls out of this country for—uh—immoral purposes?" I thought of that big Chinese behind the food vat.

"They wouldn't say something in the paper if there wasn't a truth in it. Still, there's girls that maybe just want to run away from home. Then, if the girl's folks can't find her, it's maybe easier to think the Chinese stole her than the girl got in trouble and took carbolic acid, or just wanted to run off. Hard to know."

Times like this there was more reason in Ray than made me comfortable. I wished he had more supposing in him. Then we might suppose more things together, about girls, or even immoral purposes. Might be it was because he read so many books, which didn't seem to be something he could help.

Black Butte was now a sharp outline against the sky, but the mountain still gleamed white. I closed my eyes, my sleepy thoughts wondering if Luther Burbank named his flower Shasta daisy because both flower and mountain showed white even after dark. Suddenly I blinked awake. Something in the field definitely had moved. An animal. Maybe an owl swooping to hunt. I watched the spot, eyes scratchy with hard focus. Dark had become a wall, behind which things might move and I wouldn't know. But some things I could count on: Ray was at his prayers.

15

❀ ❀ ❀

Each day we could load the rail car a little faster; each night we suffered more with the cold, the day's tiredness priming us for chill. But late on Saturday morning, after filing through the paymaster's line and pocketing our twenty dollars, we were off for one last mail pick-up at the Post Office, and from there to the grocery. Sunday would see us beating our way north before the sun had time to pink half-way down the mountain.

Early Saturday evening, stomachs full, towels over our arms and pushing our freshly loaded bikes, we headed for the washhouse. "Think we should wash by turns? One of us keep a lookout on the wheels?" I glanced at our shiny new frying pan tied to the cook sack on the back of my frame. Ray said, "Let's just chain 'em near the door." But once the bikes leaned locked against the board wall of the rough-lumber building, I gave the cook sack a final shift to tuck the frying pan out of sight.

Loud talk came at us now from inside. Grabbing our dirty clothes bundled in our shirts, we idled through the thick door held open by a rusted sadiron. The crude room was ripe with the smell of sweat and snuff and sour whiskey. In one corner several rowdies waited about a large, footed tub. We clumped across the boards, past a long wooden table and bench heavy with shoes, clothes, soaps, a bucket, combs, pipes and cinched-up tobacco bags. Two urinals, a toilet stool and a double wash-tray—where a large man scrubbed on a board—lined one wall. Another wash-tray was in use on the wall behind the big tub.

I leaned to Ray. "Purse is in my shoe."

"Watch when you take it off."

These were the same mindful men we'd worked next to all week, but this was Saturday night, enough to turn them unmindful and maybe foolish. I scootched my heel to feel the coin purse. Our trip to Seattle lay in my shoe and out there with our bikes.

The tub was stuffed with a heavy, hairy-chested man, suds boiling from his head and shoulders. Water sloshed over the oak rim of the steel tub when he shifted his weight. In our places at the end of the line, the four men ahead of us talked of sporting around in town later on. They scuffled like pups, flicking towels, teasing about what they did last Saturday night. We smiled along.

A rattleboned fellow in front of me had to be at least 6'5". "You whelps fixin' for fun tonight?" he asked. "We could see you meet a couple girls gives you a good time." Grinning, he jabbed a bony elbow in my side.

"We like to find our own girls," I said.

Ray tossed his shirt bundle in the air and caught it. "I'll wait over there, Vic," and he headed for a wash-tray behind a fellow who told us today he was an ex-stage driver.

"Ooo-eee, new fellas like to find their own girls," the tall guy repeated. The others laughed. Part of me wanted to feel like one of them. But part of me didn't, too.

"Might even know what to do with 'em once you find 'em, eh kid?" a redheaded, banty-rooster of a fellow teased. He was next in line for the tub. I nodded, then looked over to see if Ray had heard, but he was throwing his dirties into a tray.

The lanky fellow hollered to the thick man in the tub, "Hey, Mick, you scrub that head any cleaner and I'm gonna cry when I have to pile you on that stinkin' flatcar tonight with the rest of the pukey drunks." He turned and jabbed me again. The banty-rooster fellow staggered, pretending to carry a heavy load and wailed, "Peel him off the floor, carry-r-ry him to the flatcar. . . ." He gestured as to throw a body up and over. "Stack him like cordwood." The men doubled up, snorting, slapping their legs. Mick kept on scrubbing. The scraggy guy said to me, "We take turns findin' the swillbellys late Saturday night, early Sunday morning. Lay 'em two, three deep on flatcars. Haul 'em back out here. Best you not be one of 'em. Boss don't like it."

"Me and my buddy are heading out early," I told him. "We won't be going to town. . . . "

But the guy was watching a round-faced fellow readying to cuff the short man's ears, saying, "You should know, Freddie. I stacked you beside Mick last week."

The men let out their breaths and looked eager. To their delight the little fellow squared off. A third man to the side of the line cheered, "Go it husband! Go it bear!" and crouched to watch. But feisty Freddie slowly unclenched his fists, and the tight line of his mouth slackened. "The devil with all of you."

Ray now scrubbed at a washboard, as the ex-stage driver draped wet socks over the rope strung overhead. At the sidewall tray near the tub, standing crooked and slight, was the young water-pitcher lad. Stripped and scrawny, he rubbed down with a great brick of lye soap. At supper the first night we asked him his name so we wouldn't have to call him Boy when we wanted water. Joey, he told us, Joey Geller. Later he followed us outside, telling us he had no pa, and no ma since last year when he was fifteen and she died of the consumption. That night Ray and I talked about him at our campfire, agreeing his face had an unusualness, a sort of odd light seeming to come from behind it. We talked about how he said his forlorn words so they carried some of that soft light and came out sounding glad.

Of a sudden now the boy stopped his soaping and watched the tub where Mick prepared to debark. Freddie dropped his pants where he stood, readying to leap in the tub. Mick stepped out dripping—pure ox, with curly black hair a mat over most of his body. Freddie eased himself down in the sudsy water. Mick lifted his clothes from a nail on the wall, the hair on his back in tiny wet coils. Somebody mumbled, "Better get those clothes on snappy or Joey'll be after you." The words dropped on the men like a blanket, wrapping them in instant quiet. Slowly, each head turned toward Joey.

Joey had put his pants on, but still held the soap under his arm and stared, not at Mick or the tub. His gaze was fixed out through the doorway on the great white mountain, and that soft light had come up from behind his eyes to spill over his young features.

The men watched him, their faces, I thought, itching to mimic. Of a sudden, on our left flank, boots pounded the boards. I turned as the stage driver and another man and Ray joined us. Freddie sat motionless in the suds. Joey still looked out the door. I panicked.

Did the boy see somebody at our bikes? I bent to look; the load of one, handlebars of the other, just as we left them.

The ex-stage driver and the other man, both built like banded wire, walked in bowlegged deliberate steps past the tub line, eyes fixed on the now silent men. Ray stood next to me.

"All right, boys," said the stage driver. "Sounded to me and Bill like somebody was sayin' a word or two 'bout friend Mick there. Couldn't tell if the words was that Mick favored havin' folks 'preciate him bare-assed. Or was you sayin' somethin' 'bout Joey here? Him favorin' to see folks that way? Which was it, you s'pose?" The two men braced their feet wider apart, eyes repeating the gauntlet laid down.

"No need gettin' steamy, Forbes." It was Freddie, and water sloshed over the rim. "Nothin' was said we don't all of us know."

"Yeah," "That's right," "Everybody knows about Joey." The round-faced man added, "About bein' sweet on boys, that is. We just want the little bastard to know he better keep to himself."

Forbes' arms tensed, his shoulders rounding the barest bit. "Christ sake! Don't matter *who* the kid likes. Now does it?" His narrowed eyes pierced one face and the next. "Joey ever bother any o' you?" The men looked from one to another, barely shaking their heads.

The tall, skinny guy slouched a step off from the rest. "Naw, Forbes." He looked over at Joey who had moved nearer the door, his gaze still outside. "But that weaselly kid, gimpin' himself around, lookin' marshmallow eyes at us, watchin' for God to come down from Shasta Mountain. . . ." His lathy frame shuddered. "It's enough to give a man the crawls."

Ray and I traded looks. Suddenly Bill lunged, tangling into that rack of bones. The men edged back. Bill's head thudded into that high belly, buckling him. Slim stumbled, caught himself, came up clutching his middle.

My muscles were on fire, wanting to tie into one of these jokers. Ray gripped my arm hard. Freddie was climbing out of the tub, grabbing for his towel. Somebody growled, "Ge-et him."

Ray gasped, "No."

Mick shoved through, reeling one, then another fellow backward. The first about fell in the tub; the wall stopped the other; Slim faded back. Mick, flat-footed, great shoulders flexed to bread loaves, hulked around to face Bill, cordy legs rooted to the floor. Mick's chest swelled. His eyes went to slits, one scarred lid taut and shiny-pink, same as the skin of his left cheek and half his bull neck. Bill's waspy torso weaved over spindly legs. I felt sick. Ray's breath sucked in.

In a burst the moon-faced fellow exploded from around Mick. Swearing, grunting, he tore into Bill, his left clipping Bill's jaw. A fast lunge and he jabbed his doubled-up, fat knee into Bill's groin. Bill yelled and crumpled.

Ray jumped for the lardy jasper, but drew back as Forbes' fist came from nowhere to slam the jasper's big gut almost before Bill hit the floor. Forbes' hand chopped the back of the guy's neck, and he slid down like heavy cream, coming to a heap near Bill, curled up and groaning.

Mick let out a she-lion roar, grabbed Forbes and, like some terrible bird covering its young, wrapped a hammy arm around Forbes' head to smother it in a headlock. Forbes twisted in Mick's grip, rammed elbows to his middle, kicked but missed. The gnat to the elephant.

Ray had my arm in a vise. "Hold on!"

Mick's eyes widened to black marbles. Huffing, he tightened on Forbes. Forbes moaned and left off jabbing. Naked Freddie and Slim circled stealthy as coyotes. Then Freddie sent a punch to Forbes' belly.

Ray gritted, "Take Slim. I'll get Freddie."

I spun the bony fella around by his shirt, my left grazing his jaw before he knew I was there. Like a bolt his long leg flashed out, his boot driving into my thigh. I pitched backward and fell on somebody. Freddie. I was in his lap. Ray must have put him down in a famous hurry. Freddie threw me off as I jumped up, remembering my shoe. It was still on, the purse a lump under my foot.

I looked around. No Slim. Instead, striding through the doorway, the broad shape of foreman Johannson. "All right, you hellers! That been it for this night!" Johannson tugged at Mick's big arm, loosing Forbes to stagger free. But off to my left Freddie's right was smashing to Ray's face. He grabbed for the tub as he went down. I shot past Forbes, and Mick grumbling something about not wanting nobody to like his bare ass, and knelt by Ray. I lifted him to sit up. "You hurt bad?" He rubbed the side of his head. "Just tagged the tub."

With my bandanna I mopped the blood welling over his eyebrow. "It split you some. Nothing that won't heal."

He took hold of the tub to pull himself up. "You get that Slim fella?"

"He got me. Went to get him back and couldn't find him." I handed Ray the bloody bandanna. "Didn't know you could fight."

"Can't." He steadied on his heels and held the bandanna to his forehead.

Bill stood now next to Johannson, who was on his knees slapping the face of the big lard Forbes knocked cold. Behind them Mick and the fella left me his boot print were slipping out the door, Freddie right after them buttoning his pants.

During the antics I'd lost all thought of Joey. But now through the doorway, I saw the back of his dark cap and the lank of his yellow hair from under it as he sat on the steps outside. I headed that way. Ray pointed a knuckle at his forehead. "I'll give this some water and come on out."

Joey leaned his elbows on the next stair up and didn't turn at the sound of my steps, intent as he was on that mountain. This evening, hooded over by a coolie-hat cloud, it glowed more rose than orange. Forbes, hands in his pockets, leaned against the building to the side of the stairs. Hard to tell if there'd been talk between them.

"You watch the fight in there?" I asked Joey and sat on the stair beside him while I rubbed my aching thigh.

"Listen," he whispered.

"What?" I cocked an ear.

"The bell." That glad light softened his words.

"I don't hear it, Joey. Services around here get started on Saturday night?" I grinned over at Forbes. He sauntered around to sit on the bottom stair, moving as though he had never been caught in that meat press. Joey turned his head to one side and the other, muttering, but I couldn't make out what. Sounded like, "Yaktavia— Iletheleme—Yaktavia—Iletheleme," in a kind of sing-song.

"That a hymn?" I asked.

Ray put a hand on my shoulder. "Comin' through," and made his way down to sit on the bottom stair beside Forbes. He held a clean blue bandanna to his forehead.

"It's not a hymn," Forbes answered. "Joey believes what lotsa folks around here do. But he maybe needs to believe it more."

Boots clomped behind me. Johannson filled the doorway, then started down the stairs. He put a hand on the boy's head as he stepped beside him. "Little south breeze, eh there, Joey? Should be a vine night for hearing the big one." He nodded to me, Forbes, Ray. No mention of the fight. Joey had disconnected himself to vanish out there somewhere. I asked Forbes, "What is it folks believe?"

He punched a toothpick to the corner of his mouth. Slowly working it to the middle, he bit it, then spoke around it. "Some says there's two beautiful cities inside Mt. Shasta. Cities called Yaktavia and Iletheleme." I peered at the mountain with its sunset colors. "Oh, yeah?" I laughed. "Looks more like Sacramento and Stockton to me."

"Story's been around long before any of us." There was no smile in Forbes' words. "Says that deep inside the mountain are two cities of great wealth. Gold and silver used for most everything to make them more beautiful." Ray took the bandanna from his cut. "Folks really believe that?"

Shasta had lavendered; its coolie hat had become a sheer, perfect crescent over the summit. Forbes' tone was reverent. "Yaktavians are said to cast the finest bells in the universe. Some, folks say, can be found high up on Shasta. Then there's more bells inside, if you can get invited down. But that won't happen till you die. And then only if you're good enough." He looked up at Joey. "Good people like Joey's ma, they get invited down. When one of 'em in the cities wants to talk to their own around here they use the very grandest bell. That one's said to be on this northwest side."

Ray and I glanced at each other, then at Joey, his ear still tuned to the mountain. I didn't hear Bill join us, but now he sat on the top step. "Yessir." He nodded. "Many a strange and curious happening hereabouts. In my freight wagon over those spooky Siskiyous, oh-ee. . . ." His voice trailed.

"Hmmm. Many a curious happening," Forbes said softly.

A wasp hung close to Ray's face and he waved it off.

Forbes went on, "I'd say for a ma to keep carin' for a boy, him maimed when just a wee one by his no-account papa, well, seems a ma such as her might use a fine bell to let her boy know she loves him." Bath water started to run inside the washhouse, and I slid down a step so the noise wouldn't take away any words. Closer, I saw that Forbes' neck was raw, and one ear had a crust of blood. His voice so low I had to lean forward to hear, "Guess I don't figure to be smart enough to say there ain't cities under there. And maybe full of gold. Or that have big plans to improve our world up here, as story has it." Forbes roused himself to sit straighter. "Reckon the world could do without their riches sooner than without their ideas for bettering things." Louder he said, "Even those Yaktavians might have the devil's own time getting a peaceable thought wormed into a clabbered-up head like that Mick's."

"Dumb gorilla had you like a walnut in a cracker," I said and scrunched my face.

Forbes got to his feet and nodded to Bill that it was time to go. "When them trout-livered Lucifers throw darts at the boy, well, a man's got no two ways." He glanced at Joey, still sitting glisten-eyed, a small breeze playing at his shirt. Forbes spat the toothpick. "Him needin' a daddy so bad he just wants to hang around fellas, watch 'em. The kid hankers to know better who he should grow like."

Bill led Joey to his feet, and the two joined Forbes at the bottom of the stairs.

That night, out in the field, I heard an owl's hoot, and something more. A night bird or an animal probably. But its call carried a tone like none I'd ever heard, clear and vibrant, almost bell-like. Yet so distant I couldn't be certain which, bird or animal. Or if it truly was one or the other.

16

❂ ❂ ❂

These two lads, making their way to the Seattle Fair, have attracted much notice and very often the *Press Democrat* receives calls from their friends to know how they are getting along. Here is another letter: ". . . there was a gradual slope downward into Shasta Valley. This little valley is rich with cattle and grain. These results are obtained by irrigation. We passed through the small towns of Edgewood, Gazelle and Montague. From here the land became rolling."

THE *SANTA ROSA PRESS DEMOCRAT*

We slicked along, tires humming on the well-graveled, nearly level road. Travel this fine could make up for a share of the time we'd lost. Ahead, Ray passed a hay tedder and mule. In an easy rhythm I soon swayed past the assembly and yelled at the young driver, "Nice day." Behind me, he hollered, "Nice day."

North of Gazelle we stopped at a ranch where a farmer's wife forced a sack of peaches and four chicken sandwiches on us. The farmer said we should keep to every right-hand road till Montague.

I breathed deep, taking in the smell of warm sage, those dry gray bushes all about that moved stiffly in the breeze. "Yee-ii!" I shouted, letting out some romp. Ray stood on his pedals and turned to see if I was okay, while a northbound locomotive and eight cars clicked by. The engineer waved to us, and my speed just naturally picked up. "Four hundred and five miles!" I yelled. Ray stabbed an arm in the air. "Yeah-h-h!"

Mountains closed us in now, north, east, west. Our road rolled along with the country, but most of the pitches stayed easy enough to keep in the saddle, though ruts were deepening and thin dust had replaced the gravel.

As we slowed through the town of Yreka, the west range was pulling the sun down now and again, but we'd ticked off better than thirty miles this day. Past the spectators in their sidewalk chairs and around a corner, we came on a lunch wagon. A jowl-faced man leaned out the side window as we braked. On stools at the hinged counter, we ordered five pieces of apple pie, three for me, two for Ray.

"You fellas strangers in town?" asked the massive proprietor, knowing the answer.

"Wheeled up from Santa Rosa," Ray told him.

The pie was good. Not like Mama's or even Alma's or Olive's, but good.

"Men your age have to go traveling to find excitement nowadays. When I was young there was plenty goin' on right close to home. Indian fightin'." He raised his eyebrows like he hoped we'd ask questions, but our mouths were full. "Most expensive Indian our government ever mixed with, that Captain Jack," he yelled at us less than three feet away. The man was deaf. "Him and a handful of Modocs was callin' the tune for a thousand of our cavalry boys just southeast of here 'bout thirty-five years ago." He shifted his weight, and the wagon groaned.

"The Modoc War?" Ray asked, but not loud enough.

"Captain Jack and his Indians. 1873 they holed up in them lava beds," he bellowed, his middle rising and falling under his apron. "Pretty soon killed General Canby. Captain Jack was the one killed him. Shot him twice, knifed him once."

We stood up. I swiped an arm across my mouth, then thanked the fellow before Ray could start his questions.

"That'll be ten cents." The big man took a step and the wagon tilted. "Each piece."

I dug in the purse and set out a fifty-cent coin. "Fine pie, sir," Ray said, and I nodded.

When the town quit, the grade began, a steep one too. Off we got and used the ropes to steer. At the first crest we stopped under a scrub oak and munched cheese and some sweet chocolate. Shasta must be a good forty miles south now and glowed warm ivory in the late afternoon light. Chewing, I watched a bush bird flush up from a near manzanita.

Down was fast, pockets of gravel throwing the wheels, but daylight held till we reached bottom and the Klamath River. Stars had jumped out and dusk was settling. The water a powerful forty or fifty feet wide flowed inky black. Rolled up behind a boulder we were shielded from the view of road travelers. Even so, I gave a last look into the night before I closed my eyes.

Next morning, by the time the sun favored the mountaintops, we were eating trout, and Ray was telling about an old prospector he'd talked to while the two fished up stream. The fellow told about a nearby lumber town called Pokeganna that had burned to the ground a dozen years before. Ray asked him if renegades were known to use this road on the way to the border. He said sure but they most always snagged a train and not to worry.

The road coursed parallel to the river. Across, on the opposite hillside lay the Southern Pacific tracks. All three routes, water, rails, road, followed the land, bending one way and another with the meanders of the dried-up hills. Shortly after we passed the charred remains of poor Pokeganna, the road and railroad left the Klamath to head north, following to either side of a creek that led directly into Hornbrook.

On the grade out of the little town, the same eight-car train chugged north, but now sported a second engine, the double huff-huffs echoing back and forth in the canyon with such melancholy. I stopped at the crest to watch a little brown bird twit from an oak just off the road. Down the grade ahead, Ray bounced around in his considerable dust cloud. Across the canyon a burro brayed. Here, in these mountains, his call carried more sorrow than silliness. All at once lonely, I hollered to Ray, "From now on we best use our bell and whistle. Keep tabs on the other."

When I pulled alongside him at the bottom of the grade, he stretched out his hand. "Here, Vic. You carry him awhile." The billiken. "Think I need more luck than you?" I joked. Still, the little figure in my hand was in an odd way a sort of company, and I stuffed him down my blanket roll. It was time I carried the funny fellow anyway.

The afternoon was on foot pushing up grades, higher into pine and cedar country, deeper into the herbal-scented mountains. At the low point of a short downgrade we stopped at a small creek.

"Cyclometer says four hundred twenty-three," I said. "Barely twelve miles today."

"This is mountains. Twelve isn't bad. Up here dusk will be short. We best make camp."

I chained the bikes to a young pine, then with my soap was off to sluice away some dust while Ray fished for supper. Later, our feet slapping in the damp gravel at the water's edge, I followed him and the stick threaded with seven golden trout heavy on his shoulder. Beside us, the creek noised along, the water black in the shade of early evening.

"Hey!" Ray stopped in his tracks. "Who's that?"

"Who's what?"

"Somebody's at our bikes. Hey, you!" He dropped the stick and we were off at a run. But the bikes were as I'd chained them. We scanned the dusky trees, the murky undergrowth. No movement. No snapping twigs. "You sure you saw somebody?"

"I saw somebody." He eyed the saddle bags. "Unstrapped!" He shoved a hand down each one. "Revolver, hatchet, rope, here. Hey! That sack of chocolate chunks! It's gone!"

I swallowed hard. Way out here in these forlorn mountains somebody was maybe watching us right now. I squatted by my wheel, eyes probing the deepening dark.

"Whoever he is he's more interested in food than gear," Ray said.

"Whisper," I whispered.

"Why?" Ray got to his feet. "I'm thinking we can't be sure we strapped those bags. Could have been an animal I saw that got our chocolate. Thinking more, it had to be an animal. A man would have taken the gun, or the hatchet. We can't leave food that could attract—" And we headed for the fish. The stick was right where he dropped it, the seven golden trout plump and perfect. Picking them up, he carried the string to the stream and submerged and anchored the lot with three rocks. "Keep visitors from getting a whiff."

We determined to keep up a fire all night and watch by turns. I knew I couldn't sleep anyway, so took the first watch. Sitting on pine needles, I drew my knees up for warmth and to cradle the Iver-Johnson. My eyes burned from the smoke, but more from prying into the night. Up canyon an owl hooted. The creek chattered on and on. I fingered the revolver handle. How loud would a sound be before I heard it over the noise of the water? Would a renegade have time to rush me before I heard him? Would a .32 stop him? Mostly, would I shoot him? Across the creek, a pair of yellow eyes gleamed. Low to the ground they blinked out, reappearing a second later a short distance away. Another instant and they sank into the black. The cold was an ache between my shoulders and down my back. Time was a cripple, unable to move.

At last the moon came up. Nearly full, it cast shadows that swayed with the air currents. Shapes now conjured from the wall of dark. A fire might keep away creatures, but it could only help the moon to brighten Ray and me for a highwayman to see. Shivering, I rolled a half-burned log chunk into the heart of the fire where it crackled and flared. Could have been a bear stole the chocolate if we left the bag unstrapped. Bears were canny. Slapping my arms to fight the chill, I knew one thing for sure: on half the sleep we couldn't cross these mountains, much less make up the days we'd already lost. My eyelids dragged.

I reached over to shake Ray. "Hey, old buddy. Not a leaf out of place. But don't get far from the five-shot." I handed him the revolver. He groaned and sat up.

I was on watch again when the sky first lightened, then paled to green, just before pink struck the distant hills. Jays were up and squawking. Three chipmunks played tag around the trunk of a pine near Ray's head. I unfolded, set the revolver on the rock I'd leaned against and stood up, stretching myself into daytime. I mined the fish from the water and pulled the frying pan and cook sack off the bikes, all the while surveying.

The first sun slanted through the trees to glint off the frying pan balanced on the rocks over the coals. I sprinkled corn meal on the fish and laid them in the sputtering grease. Big as the pan was, only three of these beauties would fit. When the corn-mealed edges were crispy brown, I turned them. "Breakfast," I hollered. Ray grunted and pulled himself to a sit.

That was when we saw him.

17

⊛ ⊛ ⊛

We looked across the canyon. . . the railroad wound up and
up. . . in one place the track led into the side of the mountain.
On coming out the other side it turned around and tunneled
back into the same mountain and came out many feet above
the first tunnel. . . sometimes three sets of tracks one over
the other on the same mountain.

FROM THEIR LETTER TO THE *SANTA ROSA PRESS DEMOCRAT*

C rouched over the frying pan, dangling a cornmealed fish by
the tail, the boy stared at us. His curly black hair a coarse mat
to his shoulders, our highwayman was just a kid about to
steal a fish. Black eyes widening, he dropped the fish in the pan and,
like a sprung coil, leaped away. With the legs of a mustang, he took
the stream in two jumps.

"Hey, you!" I yelled, as he reached the woods. "You want a fish?"
The boy froze. Then, releasing a muscle at a time, he turned and
walked slowly back. I could imagine the grass not bending under his
feet.

"Fish?" His voice was large, carrying easily across the talky water.
He was some older than Sussinny, and but for his curly hair this lad
resembled the Indians at the fishery.

"Sure," I hollered. Again, he took the creek in two bounds.

"Company for breakfast?" Ray said beside me, revolver punched
down his belt. A few yards away the young fellow stopped. A good
half foot shorter than I was, he appeared full-grown. His firmly
developed shoulders and torso ridged under a tattered shirt held
together by one button; powerful legs were concealed in dark, sacky
trousers cinched by a leather belt black with grime and long enough
to go twice around. It was tied in a bulky knot in front, the buckle a
pendant at one end. His mass of surprisingly curly black hair would
have been a mare's nest if he hadn't bunched it into a horsetail in
back and wrapped a red cloth around it. Feet apart, arms stiff at his

sides, he was triggered to shoot off in any direction. His gaze fixed on the fish crinkling in the pan and smelling like heaven.

Ray stepped toward him and the boy tensed, ready to bolt. "You've been on our trail awhile. How come you didn't ask sooner for something to eat?"

The lad straightened. "Fish?" he said again in his man's voice. I nodded at the pan. "You fellas grab one. I'll put the rest on for seconds."

In a flick the kid snatched the biggest fish and made off with it up stream where he hunkered, half-concealed behind a boulder. Sun mirrored off the shallows beside him. Two chipmunks darted close to the rock, their striped coats glossy chestnut in the sunshine. Then over the boulder flew a perfect fish skeleton, before the boy peered around. "Fish?"

I held out my tin plate with the lovely I was about to eat. "Here." No sense making him wait. He ran to me and grabbed the fish, opened his shirt and jammed it inside. Then, before his body showed a gathering up, he was in a sprint, turned onto the road and running north.

We looked where he'd been. All that speed and the dust still in place. "Could have used him on the track team," I said and slid another trout on my plate.

"He's no highwayman, sure." Ray tossed a fish tail and bones into the stream.

By late afternoon we had walked and pushed up more grades than I wanted to count and coasted down a few short ones. To either side of the road now were stands of pines, cedars, a few firs. Sage was still thick, its bloom a stronger yellow up this high. Dust was coarse but not deep, the road narrower, the drop off the side straight down. Pushing, steering with the ropes, I hollered up to Ray stopped at the crest, "S'pose that kid circled behind us?"

"Possible. Or if he kept north, he could be across the line by now."

"Cyclometer's four hundred twenty-nine. Maybe ten miles to Oregon," I said coming alongside. "Want to try for it?"

"And straight up for nine. Too much for today." He took off.

Across the canyon, two Baldwin locomotives disappeared into a tunnel, their labored chuffs turning to dull pounds. Cars rattled outside, the tunnel gobbling them one by one. Down the grade my wheels crunched in the dirt; the Veeder counter never pinged so loud. These mountains and their quiet closed around till the most piddling sound grew to great. The sun was gone, but sweat still slid from under my cap and down my neck.

Part of me slept that night under a sizable cedar tree, but most of me stayed awake listening, watching. A full moon gave shadows to trees that moved in the shifts of air. A cougar screamed too near. I reached under my head and between my shoes. The revolver barrel felt smooth and cool. My fingers traveled into a shoe and found the ten dollars and fifty cents. In the other the billiken sat snug.

Next morning, by the time we washed our duds and ourselves, the coals from the breakfast fire had started to wink out. The day was well on. Avoiding the deep ruts, I traveled the inside shoulder, safer than outside with its sheer drop, all the while keeping a sharp eye on the bank above me for surprises. When a boy could disappear as quick as our curly-headed friend, he or another could show up just as quick. Ray pushed between the ruts, looking as unconcerned as on the road out to Sonoma after school.

Yet these dread Siskiyous were a fortress in all directions, a barricade closing us off from the world. I said, "You think the kid is a runaway from a reservation and the Indian Agency is after him? And he's maybe lurking, hoping for a chance at a couple of bikes?"

"Could be he's Modoc and not especially glad to share the same reservation with the Klamaths. Just took off to head for his home country." In a surge, I pushed ahead. Ray's reasonable sounding thoughts, so blind to worry, frayed a man's patience.

Off down the bank, did the brush jostle? I stopped, but now all was still. I dug in my side bag, felt the revolver. These far-off, lonely roads would attract most any genuine outlaw. Now in the fast-settling dusk an unusual breath-holding stillness gripped the air. I heard no bird sounds, no stir of breeze. But then my head was drifting queerly, and my muscles lagged.

"Too tired, Vic?" Ray came alongside.

"I'm fine."

He pushed out ahead.

We pressed on, around turns, down slight draws, up stiffer and stiffer grades, neither of us suggesting camp, though dusk was near to dark. A smatter of worry about bedding down in this wilderness must have taken Ray too.

Late twilight played tricks with the road and the depth of the ruts. Camp would have to be soon, at the next trickle of water, outlaws, Indians, or no. Suddenly, under me, my wheels jumped, out of control. Handlebars wrenched from my grip. "Ray!" I shouted, as I flew off. In the dark air forever, I dropped, down, down. When I hit, slamming my shoulders, back, hands, black rocks, dirt, brush rolled over me, under, around me. Then jet calm; I swam through stillness, without weight.

How much later? I climbed through the murk, reached up, fought for breath. My hand was wet, but it could move. Hurting everywhere, I dragged to an elbow. If I could find my whistle. I fumbled. No whistle on my chest, neck. I scrabbled fingers in the dirt. No whistle to call Ray. I pulled onto my side. Must not have broken anything. If only it were daylight. In a nest of brush and dirt I moved my legs, bent them, then flopped to my back like a beetle.

So far down the bank, it would be a long struggle up to the road. If I couldn't stand, I would crawl. Ray would be looking for me. In this dark he'd have some time of it. Yell, I must yell. I tried, but it came out feeble, more whimper than yell. Doubling a leg under me, I put down a hand. Pain shot through it. Use the other hand, the one not wet. Halfway to my feet I sank back. Then, a different feel took me. A presence, an animal, a person, was nearby, close. Very close. I sat up, hand throbbing, legs aching. And now my head played jokes, thinking I sensed a presence. If only I hadn't lost the whistle, the whistle to call Ray.

"You?" It was the boy, our curly-headed friend.

I felt him, heard him drop to his knees beside me. I tore myself loose from the ground, but fell back. He caught me. His hand cradled my head while strong fingers mapped it, then moved over my middle, probing, kneading. "No blood inside. Good." In a single motion his arm grasped my legs, the other my arms, and he slung me, heavier than he by half-again, over his shoulder like a shot buck. Under me, his body moved in powerful certainty through the brush, over boulders, across the scree. Too early for the moon, dark was a blanket, but the boy's feet were sure.

From above, Ray shouted, "Vic!" His bell rang.

We stopped. "Here!" the boy called.

I mouthed, "I'm okay," my breath too pushed out as he heisted me higher for a fresh grip around my legs, never losing stride. My whole self shuddered with hurts, but then my rescuer was easing me off his back and onto my legs. We were on the road.

"Vic! My gosh! And you!" Ray was beside me, grabbing the boy's arm. "Thanks, thanks."

"My bike. What happened to it?"

"Your hand. It's bleeding."

"Banged up is all."

The boy pulled at my shirtsleeve. A slash of his knife cut around the shoulder seam. He tore the sleeve off completely, using the cloth to bind my arm and hand, then tied the end strings.

"Thanks," I said. "And I don't even know your name."

"Curly John. For my hair." In the vague light I thought I saw a smile.

"Well, thanks, Curly John. I owe you a mighty big favor."

"Fish was big. Your favor. Now, my favor." There was no question, his smile spread across his face.

"Ray, my bike?"

"Found it just over the bank. Lucky it didn't follow you."

The three of us bedded down right there in the ditch by the road. In the pale light of a rising moon I drifted off to jerk awake, head throbbing, hand pulsing. If I were home there would be liniment. But then who could know if we would ever see home again.

When I blinked awake next morning the sun was a red fringe on an east mountain, the start of September 2, 1909. My arm could slow us now, but the sleeve bandage wasn't soaked through. With a grunt I lifted to my other elbow. I felt like I'd been worked over by a steel-levered harrow. Ray still slept. But at my head, in the empty ditch where Curly John had bedded down, was a flat boulder. On it lay my whistle and cord; beside them our imp of a billiken sat catching the first pink hints of day.

18

❁   ❁   ❁

Dear Hazel:

How is the little sister getting along? Just think where your brother is—almost to Washington. There are lots of little girls in this country about your age. They make me think of you. Your "Buddy." Victor.

FROM A PENNY POSTCARD

The way old Curly John's feet carry him, he could be loping along those hills by this time." I nodded toward the mountains off to the east.

"Maybe near to the Lost River country, Modoc lands." Ray sat in the road, bike parts in a fan around him, and daubed Vaseline on a brake spring, adding, "Wherever he is, he's our friend."

"None better," I agreed and loosed the bandage on my hand, unsticking it where the blood glued.

Maybe forty minutes later, after a sharp bend at the bottom of a draw, we splashed through a shallow run of water. Once across, we turned to look up at a large board sign facing the other way. Big black letters declared: CALIFORNIA'S NORTHERN BOUNDARY. We clapped each other on the back. "All the way to Oregon," I hollered to Ray right next to me. "We made it, Vic! Clear to here." I started to clap him on the back again but he was bowing his head, so I bowed mine too.

At a catch of water, my eyes still fastened on the sign, I squatted and undid the bandage. Jaw clenched from the bite of the water, I worked the flesh, cleaned out the dirt, then let the blood seep, as I tried to concentrate on a skater bug, his water circles breaking water circles breaking water circles. Alongside, a covered rig and team of four eased up, the lead animals bending to water while the second span stamped dust as they waited. Soon the driver yelled "Hee!" and the first span lumbered ahead so's the second could water.

On the push up our first Oregon hill my head pounded like an engine, and I stopped to rub the goose egg on my forehead. Ray, beside me, said, "If Roy Ripley could see you now, clothes in tatters, bloodied up, he'd turn you into a cartoon for the *Call Bulletin* sure." I smiled to think of our old Santa Rosa school chum. Miss O'Meara, our teacher, used to tell Roy he didn't have to do the same work as the rest of us. "It's just fine if you illustrate the lesson instead of writing it out," she'd say, which provoked the rest of us. Roy was his real name, before he took his big job at the San Francisco newspaper and started signing his cartoons Bob Ripley.

On the other side of the canyon a southbound train stood stopped and puffing just outside a tunnel. Ray uncapped his canteen and swigged. "Must be tunnel thirteen."

"Tunnel thirteen?"

"Railroad summit. Remember old Bill? At Weed? Told us that's where they do a brake check before going down the California side."

"Hmm," I said, not remembering. Around the next turn, letters on a small board sign nailed to an oak tree spelled: SUMMIT. Ray pulled out his watch and flipped open the case. "3:15 p.m. September 2, 1909." I bent over the cyclometer. "Four hundred fifty-two."

And we threw our legs over the bikes for the coast down. "Fully fif-te-en miles a-way from a bed and a good square me-eal." I belted the old song as though God himself were hard of hearing.

Braking, I followed Ray, each of us riding the outside shoulder, his boil of dust bad enough I pulled my bandanna up over my nose. At the first bridge he jumped off and laid his bike down on the planks. "Time for trees." "I'll chop," I yelled, in charge. "You switch the ropes front to back," and I dug the hatchet out of a side bag.

Across a rocky clearing in a stand of firs, I swung with my good hand and let fly a whack near the base of a thick sapling. The blow rang strong and clear, the only sound on the mountain. Strength in me was twice that of a month ago. As the tree toppled, I lammed into a second, that instant bringing on me a queer kind of knowing. Not a pride exactly, more a quiet certainness, as though the universe was my friend and whatever man or nature put in my path I could now figure a way past. My chest was full of breathing and this knowing, the two partnering to lift me higher than I stood. It was as though, for the first time, I had met the person I truly was. And I could trust him.

Saplings secured behind the bikes, we were on our way down the long coast north where a wide valley now lay bathed in late yellow light. My tree yanked and let up, tugging the wheels right, left. Warm stickiness welled in my left palm. Across the canyon, past a massive rock overhang, the famous Dollarhide trestle's timber struts were delicate tracery spanning the gorge, and we stopped to marvel.

Down, down, the road was a snake. Ahead now, Ray was nowhere to be seen. Even his dust had settled. Then, around a turn the road leveled and there he was, astride his wheel talking to a fellow in front of a weathered building that had to be the Dollarhide Toll-road House. Ray hollered as I pulled up in my own dust cloak, "Thirty-five cents. Each."

I swung off, reached down the blanket roll for the coin purse and handed the man three two-bit pieces. He dropped the coins in the breast pocket of his shirt and handed me a nickel. "Been long on the road?"

"Nearly a month, sir," Ray said.

I added, "On our way to the Seattle Fair."

"Couple of fellows passed through here a time ago that'd been to the fair. Talked about that Forestry Building. The one held up by 124 logs. Made it up there with a good wagon and two healthy horses. Just wheels between you and the road, that'll be some big trip, lads. Three months now and no rain. It's overdue. Roads here can wash right out from under you." He shook his head as he turned toward the house where a young girl on the stoop stood watching. She looked to be about seven, my sister Hazel's age.

Back on the road the air was warmer the lower we dropped. The valley below was a quilt of green orchards and yellow fields, and in the deep shade of a high west hill were breasted buildings that must be Ashland. Lower yet, we made camp next to a drowsy little creek, all the while complaining about the heat and mosquitoes.

A rooster launched us into our first Oregon morning, his crow just as jolting as any in California. After washing ourselves and our underwear we were on the road eating biscuits and jerky, my bandage looped on the back of the frame, underwear draped over the crosspiece where I could hide it handily as we rode through town.

The day promised to be a scorcher, and at the town park we sat against trees to drink from our canteens. Three young women walked past, never glancing our way. Yet, of a sudden I was self-conscious. Digging down the blanket roll, I said, "I'm taking six-bits. Gonna buy you pants with two legs and me a shirt with both sleeves," and nodded at a dry goods store across the street.

Later I ambled back in a stiff gray shirt and swung a feed sack with pants for Ray, oatmeal and chocolate pieces. I said to him hunched over the writing tablet, "We got seven dollars and eighty-five cents left."

"Won't take us to Portland. Gonna have to find work."

Out of town the road was badly chewed up and mighty rough going. We soon came on the reason: a locomotive traction engine with a regular stack and boiler, huffing like a train and pulling seven mammoth wagonloads of gravel. We passed wagon after wagon until finally, alongside the engine and the wheel-claws digging deep into the road surface, we waved to the driver in the open cab. He waved back, but no smile.

Now the road was smooth, and we rode side by side. Those Siskiyous safely behind us and a fresh north breeze to face into, my insides wanted to laugh. So I busied my head for a funny thing to say so Ray would laugh with me, when, under me, an explosion! My rear wheel lumped around, then wobbled out of control. I gripped the handlebars hard, pain stabbing my left palm, but stopped before I was thrown.

"She tore bad on you." Ray was beside me.

The casing was loose from the rim for a full quarter turn; the tube had blown a nasty four-inch hole. I wrapped the bandage around my bleeding hand, and we set to work. "Casing's weak," he said, pasting on glue. "Probably means more trouble." Our spare was a throwaway from Santa Rosa days. We hoped not to have to test our luck against it, so installed the patched tube back in the same casing and hoped. Surface here was splendid oil and gravel, but we would pedal slow anyway.

Ray passed a wagon and I followed. "Good day," the driver called. A small boy between him and his wife played "You're a Grand Old Flag" on the mouth organ. "G'day," I hollered back. Soon we overtook a hay wagon, a couple of young farmers on the seat and three more in the bed sitting on bales. Friday night must be a busy time in Medford to judge from the traffic. Through town Main Street told the answer: colored banners stretched from one side to the other announced Ringling Brothers Circus.

"Might be we could get on at the circus," I said, remembering the times I'd carried water for the elephants so I could see the circus in Santa Rosa.

"We need money, not circus passes." He was right, of course. Still, I didn't answer him.

Out of town, the valley was broad and level. Good-looking grain farms lined the road on either side. Just past the settlement of Central Point I felt the casing give only a moment before the tube burst. I jumped off. The bike flopped, front wheel spinning, the rear tire gone to glory. After we'd layered bicycle tape on the casing's weakest places and mounted the spare, a serious-minded border collie from a farm house near the road caused enough commotion that the farmer strode toward us from the barn.

"Trouble?" he yelled over the barking. A big man, his middle shoved his suspenders well off to the sides.

"A flat, sir," Ray told him. "Fixed now. We'll be moving on so's your dog can quiet."

"Pay no mind to old Gretchen." The farmer's heavy shirt was spattered with dark stains that looked like blood.

"The wife's setting supper out. You're welcome to eat, bed down in the loft."

"Thanks, sir," we said together.

Inside the barn a young spike hung on a block and tackle from a cross-timber. The farmer gave the carcass a half turn and lifted the head by its antler. Dark oozes dripped from the slashed neck into the sickeningly sweet-smelling pile of straw below, it already heaped from the gutting. The farmer wiped his hands on his pants and headed for the pitchfork leaning against a stack of bales. "You men clean up at the pump. I'll be along."

But Ray grabbed the pitchfork. "I'll just pitch up this fouled straw for you, sir." So I aimed for the wheelbarrow. "If you'd show me where the compost is, sir? We'll be in shortly."

Later, at the table, his wife, almost as big as her husband, laughed up from her belly as I told of our goings-on in the way I had of turning things funny, and she pressed us to take seconds and thirds of the roast beef and mashed potatoes.

Bedded down in the warm straw that night, the moon knifing through wide cracks in the barn siding, sounds were only a now and then thump from the stalls below and a faint scrinch of rope as the carcass swung from the timber.

"Your tube and taped-up casing won't make it far, Vic. S'pose your dad could get Acme Cyclery to make good on that tire?"

"Won't hurt to try," I drawled sleepily, wishing it had been my idea.

Next morning we pedaled back to Medford as the early sun glossed new-bundled hay and brightened the long stretches of yellow mallow near the road. Behind the counter at the Wells Fargo Building, a clerk with arm elastic and green visor took my message: "Dear Papa, . . . If these are guaranteed, please send replacements to Roseburg, Oregon."

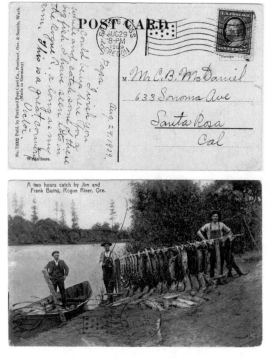

A two hours catch by Jim and Frank Burns, Rogue River, Ore.

Out of town and again passing the ranch, we saw no one, not even Gretchen. I led, pacing slow. On the tracks no more than thirty feet away a short train overtook us, and the engineer waved and smiled.

At a bridge across the great Rogue River we stopped to lean over the rail and sniff the fishy air. "One of those fish wants catching, Vic." I gave him a look and remounted. "And you with no Oregon license and an aim to be a high-wrought minister."

"Placer action," he said, pretending to be lost in a study of the hill in front of us. There, large chunks were gone from the earth, leaving gray-red gouges among the oak and madrone.

"Uh-huh," I agreed, as though I'd known.

Through the little town of Gold Hill, past the livery stables and Western Union, the Gold Hill News, and the blacksmith shop, all rowed up, the buildings looked to be from the sixties all right, the years those gold-seekers ripped open the hillside.

Dustier, ruttier now, the road was hard going. A fine lot of mud this would stir up if the rains came. Late light turned the narrow valley a gold-green, while behind us clouds were the color of bright lead where the sun targeted their bellies, bellies full to bursting. Standing on the pedals, I tried for more speed, but my wheels grew roots.

Outside the settlement of Rock Point Ray slowed. "Look for a place to bed down?" I nodded. But beyond the bridge west of town the road smoothed, its gentle ups and downs easing in and out of the hills' skirt folds, and we kept going. Then ahead, thud! Crack!

Ray angled sharply, bike weaving before it crumpled under him like a done horse. He hopped off and grabbed the wheel front and back to hold it up. "Weld gave out!" Beside him, I gripped his crossbar, parted from the down tube. He dropped on his knees, fingers moving over the lower part of the tube. "Fractured here too."

"Happened when the weld broke, likely. Strain was too much." I could see daylight through almost half the tube. Another second under his weight would have snapped it. I plopped in the dirt. "Damn! Damn it!" Insult on insult, big fat raindrops now spat on the bike's metal. All around us dust tufted up in little bursts. "Damn it!" I heard from the other side of the bike. From Ray!

19

❀ ❀ ❀

Dear Papa:

I wish you could be up here for awhile and catch some of these big fish. I have seen lots in the Rogue River as long as my arm. This is great country. Victor.

FROM A PENNY POSTCARD

Discouraged, I gave up trying to splint Ray's broken frame with a pine branch and bicycle tape. One break I might have gotten away with. Not two.

"I couldn't quick-do the bike," I hollered as he scrambled up the bank, grinning big as he held by the gill a glistening trout that had to be more than two feet long. "Not illegal before the Lord, I think," he said, but canted his head in the way he had when the devil took him. Sometimes I had real hopes for this friend of mine.

Later, as we bedded down on the ground warmed by the coals, the darkening twilight sank to a fearful black, but turned less fearful by the cheerful sing-song of the river. Ray tossed and made fretting noises, finally waking himself up. "You asleep?"

"Nah," I said.

"We'll have to push and carry the wheels to Grants Pass."

"Looks to be only about six miles on the map. Rain's over, seems. Still, might do better on the tracks than slogging through mud."

"Six dollars and thirty-five cents won't be enough to braze my bike and buy tube and casing for yours."

"Worries look better in daylight, Ray." Something scurried through the pine needles past my head. "One thing, tube and casing'll last longer pushing than riding. I should make it to Roseburg."

I was awake till after the moon came up, it looking all pounded down and casting but faint light. Still, enough to see a bat zag and streak before it disappeared. Daylight was a time away, yet outlines began to come strangely plain. Suddenly my nostrils smarted, and I jumped up. The sky had brightened, but behind a heaviness of—my God, smoke! "Ray! Get up!"

A dense cloud stifled the valley and lay over the river. An unhealthy red festered in the northwest sky.

"Forest fire!" he rasped, on his feet. The acrid taste and smell of the air made my stomach roll. "Other side of the north hill, looks like."

"For a wonder the road and rails run just about east to west through here."

I licked a finger and held it up. "Practically no wind. Oughta do fine. Blaze could be spent by now. Glow and smoke last after the fire's used up." I didn't want to wonder did I truly believe what I said. My nostrils stung; smoke was thickening. Half an hour later and a quarter of a mile down the path beside the tracks, daylight was a burdened amber haze. Pines and madronas to either side were tinged gray with the ash that now sifted down, it clinging to our clothes and mouths and noses and coating the ground the color of soft death.

Ray stopped, supporting both ends of his bicycle against him in a way that the tape wasn't strained. "Bandannas, Vic." He untied his from around his neck. I did the same, and we masked our noses and mouths. From above his handkerchief he surveyed the north hills. "Fire's still on the other side. But if it comes over and the wind doesn't change, fire could crown down fast. We'd have a run to make it out of here."

We walked fast. "Wind seems westerly." I angled my head to get a sense of how the ash came down. A breeze swirled bits of gray powder in front of us, then clouded in a sickly veil. We ran now, carrying the wheels, bandannas over our faces, eyes blinking from the sting and grit.

The wind changed. Now it was from the north. Ray hollered back, "Crews should be coming along. Then we'll be fighting fire with 'em." Laboring for breath, running, I choked as two mighty explosions, one after the other, came from up the hill. Ray coughed and shouted, "Trees!" just as another blast tore through the smarting grit that passed for air. "Fire must be just over the ridge."

I let the bike down to bounce, hefted it again and ran faster, nostrils burning, eyes streaming. Morning light was brown now, unreal. An explosion, louder. Orange streaked the ridge-top, tracing awful arcs. Sparks and bits of flame glittered in a scatter. Another blast and flames and smoke jetted high, falling, spilling down the hill, igniting flames there and there. Ahead, a doe crashed through the brush and plunged across the tracks, neck stretched long and wild. A two-prong buck and a doe with what looked like a great burned patch in her pelt leaped high through the brush toward the river. Behind them waddled a black bear, rump rolling side to side. We ran, bikes bumping down, coughing, tears burning. Ray yelled, "If the fire gains on us, we'll go for the river too."

"I'll let you know when," and I glanced behind me. The skyline was traced with red-orange comets. A ball of fire belched up to land in a treetop, blossoming there. Islands of flame towered on this side now, fire bursts exploding from them. Bark soared, branches flew, fresh fire islands flared. Smoke seeped among the trees and brush, and streamered over the river. All around now, a stormy sort of rushing noise hissed over the low growl of the feeding fire. Crying, running, I shouted, "Where's that crew?" For the first time a sick warmth crawled up the back of my neck and arms. "Ray! To the river!"

A chunk of flaming bark landed in a sputter of sparks not ten feet away. A bit of flame faltered, then ripped all ways at once. "River!" I screamed. He looked over his shoulder just as a blast of—wind?—hit my face. For an instant I breathed clean air. Another gust. Was the wind truly from the west? Ray had felt it too. "Keep to the tracks!"

As if the fire's terrible force had created its own weather, wind from the west came now in a fury. Bucking into it was a fresh fight; ash blew in my eyes, stung my face. But no dread warmth lay on my back. Clean air lashed me, pushed at the bike, the load. Still we ran, and ran, putting more, more distance between us and that firestorm.

Around a sweeping bend, the tracks led into flat valley land. Out there oaks and pines stood clothed in green; bark on the madronas was a lusty red. Wind quieted. My breath came deep and full as I slowed to a walk and set my bike on the path.

Ray stopped, unscrewed the cap of his canteen and gulped. "Now, the wind should hold."

"Put God to work on it, Ray."

He smiled. "Who do you think sent the wind in the first place?"

I wondered if he even remembered this was Sunday. But then Ray didn't forget things like that.

20

❀   ❀   ❀

So far we have covered but a third of the distance through
this state, as the roads are so rough and hilly that we cannot
do as well as expected. . . . We have traveled on everything
from rocks covered with corn stalks to the famous corduroy
roads. . . . We haven't had as much as a quarter of a mile of
level road since we left Grants Pass.

FROM THEIR LETTER TO THE *SANTA ROSA PRESS DEMOCRAT*

Back on the road, it gentled down into the sleepy little town of
Grants Pass couched in a bowl of the mountains. Stores were
buttoned tight and the ladies and gents walked erect in their
good duds on their way to church. We headed for the town park
where we'd have our own day of rest and a better try at keeping our
sorry-looking selves out of folks' sight. Come morning we'd be
waiting for that brazier soon as he put key to lock.

By two-thirty, Monday afternoon, September 6, the swarthy
German brazier had mended Ray's frame with two bright shiny
welds and collected our four dollars. "Might giff in another place,"
he told Ray strapping the bags back on his wheel. "But she neffer
giff on you in those same places, effer agin." Around three we were
pushing up the steep incline of the road north, Ray between the
ruts, me on the inside shoulder, slender as it was. Off to the east,
smoke no longer plumed and erupted, but still lay thick and blue.

"Good to have my wheel of a piece again," Ray said, hardly
puffing.

"Sure hated to give that fellow our last three-dollar gold piece
though," I said, more out of breath than I wanted him to know.

A horse and cart rounded the turn ahead, and we pulled off for
the old fellow. I wondered if his boxes of squash and corn had been
only half full when he started out, or if the vegetables had flown
loose on the road. I'd keep an eye off to the sides just in case.

The cut of our road ahead showed here and there through the
oaks and pines, each time higher up than the last. Back to plodding,

I small-talked, "What's the name of that new Portland mayor? Going to turn it into an open town?"

"Simon, I think. Might not be open yet though, so don't get ideas."

In the draw before the next up grade, the road was surfaced with crosswise logs and dirt smattered between. "Corduroy," Ray announced, thumping and bumping over them.

"How d'you s'pose they stay put in winter?" I glanced up the channeled ravine.

"Logs are different lengths. Dirt fill'd seat 'em for a season or two."

Sixth Street, Grants Pass, Oregon

A half hour or so farther and higher we came to an unmarked fork and stood there wondering before we pushed out onto the right fork, the broadest with the most traveled ruts. A full hour up the rocky road we came on two mines. Farther yet, a lumber mill which had shut down for the day. Shortly, the road ended.

"More lost time," I fumed and faunched, as we about-faced.

Finally back on the first road, darkness already claimed the thick growth under the fir forest. Ray said, "Camp?" "Do better with water," I said, wanting to be the one to decide.

The north wind picked up now, a tussle to push against even on foot, and the sky was suddenly dark with heavy, pewter-colored clouds. Lowering light made it harder to find the shoulder, so we took to the ruts. The road even fell away on the outside now and then, narrowing it to scant wagon width. A sharp gust yanked at my bedroll, wrenching the bike in my grip. Ray lighted his lamp. I did the same, but they gave bobbling circles of light, catching as much off to the side as on the road. Suddenly, the mountain across canyon flared white, giving shape to the trees. Behind us, thunder rumbled.

"Clouds'll spill soon. Want to stop?" I hollered.

"Bottom can't be far," he yelled back. So we pushed and bumped, fighting the wind and the fir branches that swirled through

POST CARD.

THIS SPACE MAY BE USED FOR CORRESPONDENCE

THE ADDRESS ONLY TO BE WRITTEN HERE.

Mrs Ella McDaniel
633 Sonoma Ave
Santa Rosa. Cal.
Sonoma County.

Oregon County Road.

the air. The rain could miss us. Dump somewhere else. Another flash, brighter than the last, on our side of the canyon. Thunder blasted on the instant lightning flooded the sky. "Ray!" I yelled. "Off the road!"

"Lights ahead." he hollered back. At once the world was still, windless, holding its breath. Then splat and splat, another and another, large drops, faster, harder. In the time it took to think it, rain poured from a thousand spigots, daggers with the points down. Road dust exploded like shell bursts and smelled of wet dirt. Soaked, I ran after Ray. Drops were fewer but still the size of young peanuts. Lightning opened the sky full of tumbled, inky billows, but the roar of thunder was, thankfully, some distant.

Across a short plank bridge a scatter of lights a quarter of a mile or so off looked to be a small settlement. We made camp next to what we learned in the morning was Wolf Creek. Rain became a drop here, there. We were too tired not to sleep. Next morning, draping my still-wet clothes over the bike frame, I glanced at the Veeder. "Yesterday only twenty miles."

Ray grunted, and we set out.

Wolf Creek's inn and stage stop was grand, with three front doors and two porches. Morning air was crystal clean after last night's scrubbing, and the sky shone like the washed blue of Mama's china bowl. Up a short grade we were off, picking our way through the storm's harvest of boughs and limbs.

After several miles mostly on shank's mare, Ray stopped to wait for me where the road opened onto a pretty valley. "Never saw a surface like this before, Vic." The road across the valley was covered with crosswise corn stalks several deep, a surface designed to keep folks' rigs from miring in the mud. When I dug a shoe toe through the stalks I hit rock, rocks placed with the flat side up. All this made for toilsome walking, having to lift the bikes enough the wheels could turn.

"Corn stalk road. Something to write Finley about." Ray chuckled. "Santa Rosa'll think we're flimflamming 'em sure." His chuckles now, us needing to heft our wheels, to dawdle time we didn't have, put a sudden botheration in me. "Many corn stalk roads and we can forget that ten million dollar fair, Ray." But he wouldn't rise to my bother and said, "Ten million dollars. You know why, Vic? 'Cause it's ten years since the first Klondike gold ship arrived in Seattle, that's why."

"Hmm," I said. But the morning sun did feel grand on my back, and to either side of the road the swaying heads of rose-blue mallow on their tall stems reminded me of how much Mama liked wild flowers.

Once across the valley the road angled up sharply but was of dirt again. "I miss the trains," I hollered, sniffing a skunk. "Map shows the tracks several mountains to the west," Ray yelled behind me.

"Hey!" I pointed to a huge fallen fir across the road ahead, its massive trunk and thicket of limbs creating a barricade the size of a locomotive. "Up and over?" Ray suggested. "I'll climb first. Hand me a bike. I'll perch it in the branches. We'll relay 'em."

By the time we reached the summit we'd clambered over and through four white pines and that first fir. The downgrade was slow too, but only because of rocks and ruts. At a plank bridge crossing a narrow draw we stopped just to laugh at the sign posted to the side of the road: *Five Dollars Fine for Driving Faster Than a Walk.* The sign was a usual one, of course, but here, now, after lugging and hefting our wheels over cornstalks and trees, it was too funny. Shortly, after eating a couple of apples, we crossed the bridge, running so we'd violate the law. Dusk was settling when we reached Canyonville where we camped beside Elk Creek. Ray caught a couple of big ones, and we lost no time putting them between sticks.

Next morning we kept seat to saddle almost from the time we started out. As I passed Ray I hollered, "You know how many prohibition towns there are in Oregon?" Do him a fair amount of good to learn that what he didn't know amounted to a sight more than what he did. But catching up, he said, "Oregon doesn't decide by towns like California does."

"So? No prohibition?"

"They vote by counties. More prohibition counties than not in Oregon, I think. Washington, only a few wet towns. Seattle's one.

You can drink all you want when we get to that fair." He laughed so loud a woman leading a cow along a path several hundred yards ahead looked around, and I said, "Better watch these rocks."

He knew well enough I used to go in the Santa Rosa saloons for a free lunch, but he forever teased that I went in for a drink. The times I did have a whiskey I never told him about.

The road followed the South Umpqua River, a ponderous bullsnake of water, with an every now and then rowboat carrying a fisherman or two. Soon we had the railroad with us again, the tracks first on our side of the river, then across. Miles were easier to come by this day. The sun was dipping under the western hills when we first saw Roseburg, a sizeable town, spread before us in a valley.

"We'll go to the Post Office tomorrow," I said. "See if Papa sent a tire."

"Might try for a couple of days work here, Vic. Two dollars and thirty-five cents won't get us through."

We camped between the road and the river, almost too tired to be happy about the day's thirty-seven miles.

21

❀   ❀   ❀

Dear Alma:

How is school? Tell Mama I am still well and haven't starved yet..
..Lost two days waiting for the tire to come from Santa Rosa.
Just hope now we can make it to Seattle in time for the fair.
Victor.

FROM A PENNY POSTCARD TO HIS SISTER

Next morning, after a yank at some jerky we were on the road, the sun already a burden, carried as it was on air heavy with moisture. Halfway down the hill to town my tire let loose, the tape we'd used to hold it together flapping, the tire thumping to shreds. I sat on my heels and scowled at the mangled mess. Ray came back, groaned and said, "Guess we're lucky the thing held together this long."

"No use to fix it. Tire could be waiting in town."

Walking the bike down the hill, tags of tape and rubber slapping the road, I couldn't help but consider. Ray and his praying gave me powerful irritation now and again, but times like this made a man pause. If the tire had given up during that storm in the dark, or a lot of other places I could think of, we'd have had a prize problem. A man could wonder if such a coincidence truly was a coincidence, or if Ray's being on good terms with his Lord might just tip the scales to our side.

But the tire wasn't at the Post Office. Worse, who knew if it ever would be. Shambling out to the sidewalk, grateful for the shade of the awning, we stood there sorting through our mail and misery. I swabbed sweat from my face and neck as I scanned letters from home. Papa got my wire, but hadn't talked to the cyclery yet.

"Want to look around?" Ray broke through. "See if there's work?"

"Could work a day or two, I guess. No more though, tire or no tire."

"Have to work sometime somewhere," he said, too reasonably. "Sooner if we have to buy a tire."

We walked the bikes back down the street we came in on, stopping in the block where most of the buildings had lately burned to the ground.

"Hey, what's going on?" And Ray turned down Jackson Street where a crew was spreading gravel. Behind them, a steamroller snorted and crunched over it. "Want to see if we can get on?"

"Hot work," I said. "A mill might put us under a roof." But Ray wasn't listening. "There's the foreman." And he was off toward a fellow wearing a tie and carrying a tablet. We were hired.

"You men get your shovel and rake from Pete there at the gravel wagon," the foreman loudly instructed over the noisy roller and the scatter and scrape of gravel. The man's accent was thick as the air was muggy, and sounded Slavic. "Work off Nick's cart there. He hauls from the wagon. Only Nick to load the gravel, hear? Do what he says. Fellas, you hear me?"

"Yes, sir," we chorused.

Two stores away, near enough to keep an eye on, we locked the bikes to a hitching post at the curb. Pete grunted as he handed us a scoop shovel and a wide rake from a stack of tools in the wagon bed. Then he jumped down to tighten a hitch on one of the two broad-rumped Percherons. Swarthy-skinned and dark-haired, Pete might not speak English at all.

Nick was a short, beef-shouldered fellow with snapping black eyes that barely glanced at us as he swung his shovel-load up out of the cart to cast the very coarse gravel over the road. Alongside him, Ray dug into the heap of broken rock. I began raking the jagged chunks across the black, soft bitumen. With arms the size of saplings, Nick shoveled in a strong, steady rhythm, broadcasting each heavy load over a swath of street as easily as I'd strew chicken feed.

In this canyon between buildings, heat congealed on the skin and singed the nostrils. Air was too heavy to move and no breeze to make the try. Breathless heat, the acrid smell of warm petroleum, and dust clouding from every shovel cast was as sure-enough an imitation of hell as any live man should ever know. Sweat bubbled from under my cap. I wanted a swig from my canteen more than I'd ever wanted anything, but I couldn't stop before I'd started.

Paving Jackson Street in Roseburg, Oregon, for the first time, 1909.
Photograph courtesy of Douglas County Museum

Ray's shovel-loads were scant, and he threw unevenly, so I
worked more behind Nick. The roller's giant cylinders ground
along after me, the engine chuffing. Every two or three shovels-full
Nick pushed the cart ahead, a part of his rhythm. Ray's face had
redded up, a worry.

"Take the rake awhile. We'll switch off," I said and blew at the
droplets dripping off my nose.

He straightened and handed me the shovel. A few shovel-loads
proved I was sadly out of shape from the waist up. I lifted more
rock than Ray but only about half what Nick threw. My throat was
dry as a pelt on a fence. I took a pull on the canteen, but Nick
looked square at me, scattering his load the while. I hurried the
canteen to my pocket and dug in the shovel.

Our caps set us apart from the others with their wide-brimmed
hats, but no amount of brim would shunt this heat; they swam in
their sweat same as Ray and I. While Nick plowed back to the
wagon to fill the cart, we mopped ourselves and switched tools
again. No knowing which action was harder, but this gave different
muscles the chance to complain. Ray pulled out his watch. "Fifteen
minutes till lunch time, Vic. Hang on."

The foreman finally blew his whistle. Nick straightened and leaned his shovel against the cart. "You have food?" His accent was easier to understand than the foreman's. Greek, I decided. Looked to be an all-Greek crew. We told him we had lunch on the bikes. "Be back in half hour," he ordered and headed for the gravel wagon along with the others.

Pete had taken a tarp off a pile of lard pails near the wagon seat. The men grabbed them and moved off to sit on the curb or stand in groups, talking in their tongue, laughing, gesturing. We still had some cheese and apples and raisins, but before eating we stepped in to Josephson's store and asked if we might fill our canteens. The portly proprietor sent us out back where Ray pumped first while I drank and doused my head, then his turn.

After lunch the heat held us fast, rising from the street, gripping sideways off the buildings. My shirt, undershirt, trousers stuck to me. If I hadn't tied my bandanna around my forehead I wouldn't have been able to see for the waterfall. And my senses swirled about in my head. But I couldn't pass out. Not around all these men. Why didn't Ray look done in? His face was barely flushed now. My thoughts came hard, wanting to disappear on me. Was it a fact that a man's brains could truly leak out through his sweat, as some said? If they did, was I eating my own thoughts when I licked the brine that trickled into my mouth? I had no real idea of time—how long I'd shoveled, how long I'd raked.

At last, the foreman's shrill quitting whistle. Close to nausea, I straightened, a piece at a time. My head ached like a split gourd. Both hands were badly blistered. And I'd never be able to move my arms or shoulders again.

"Vic. Ray," Nick said. His black eyes snapped with maddening energy. "Tools into the wagon. You be here tomorrow?" I sagged inside and glanced at Ray. He looked tired but not vanquished and said, "We'll be here." I winced. "Might just be for the morning, Nick." And to Ray, "We'll check the Post Office at noon."

"Four of us have house by big maple tree. Next street." Nick pointed east. "You eat with us tonight? Seven o'clock?" Before Ray could refuse, I said, "Thanks."

At six forty-five we were leaning our bikes against their front porch. Nick met us at the door and introduced us to Pete, who grunted again, and two more olive-skinned men. The older one they called Pop, and Christos, a slender fellow busy in the kitchen. Nick gestured us to sit on benches at a long plank table and handed us each a glass of dark amber liquid. "Beer, "he said, his own glass filled with a milky liquid. "I think no *ouzo* for you." Pete and Pop settled themselves on a bench. From a large pitcher they watered their *ouzo*, turning their drinks cloudy.

Ray set his glass in front of me. "My friend here'll drink for both of us."

Sitting by Ray, Nick said, "A man makes choices." For an apron Christos had tucked a towel in the top of his overalls and tied a cord around his waist. He clomped from the range to the counter to the long worktable carrying dishes and green vegetables. All the while he clenched under his arm a knife the size of a cutlass. As the men refilled their glasses, their talk grew louder. "You new here?" Pop hollered.

Ray said, "Wheeling to Seattle, to the fair up there."

"Must be fine life." Pop didn't look at us.

Nick said, "Our crew pave all of Roseburg town."

"Umm," I said. Roseburg would have macadamed streets before Santa Rosa. Ray and I had sweated buckets to help an Oregon town come in ahead of our own.

Ray said to Pop across the table, "Our home town paper is sending us on the trip. We write letters that they print." I couldn't figure why he needed to explain anything to the old man. Pop looked up and glared at Ray, then me.

"The boys work like men," Pete said, as to excuse us. Pop lowered his eyes for a long moment, then grabbed his glass and drank lustily. Nick got up to go to the table where Christos chopped vegetables, returning with two large crusty bread rounds. "Poppo he thinks only Greeks know how to work." Nick passed the bread rounds, but kept a watch on the old fellow sitting hunched over now, the muscles of his scraggy jaw in spasms. Ray seemed anxious, talking fast. "Americans are not so different from Greeks, all taken to account."

"Food it comes," Christos said.

Suddenly Poppo jumped to his feet, black eyes taking up most of his wizened face. He struck a fist with bread in it hard on the table. "Americans same as Greeks? You hear?" The old fellow looked wildly from Nick to Pete to Christos who now set two platters on the table then sat down next to Ray. Pop yelled something in Greek, his gray hair trembling.

"Sit, Poppo. The boys good workers."

"I don't eat here." Grabbing what was left of a round of bread and his glass of *ouzo*, the old fellow stomped out of the kitchen.

"I didn't mean to rile him," Ray said, stricken. Through a mouthful Pete said, "Pop still lives in a few years ago. You pay no mind." Nick said, "Down at Riddle south of here. People say Poppo shot the foreman's wife. Poppo told them no. Everybody was shooting."

"Why was anybody shooting?" I asked, helping myself to a slab of lamb.

"We work for Southern Pacific," Pete said. "Lay steel on the track. Live in boxcars. One day after work, after we hung up six sheep outside, we just in from blowing hide off them and it's time for dinner." Christos bent sideways to get Ray's attention. "First stick pipe stem in sheep, behind fore leg, then blow." He pursed his lips and blew. "Slips off like skin from the grape." His lean face split into a wide smile.

"Sheep has nothing to do with Poppo's story." Nick's black eyes squinted. "Outside box car Poppo on guard that night. People not like Greeks. They blast our ovens where we bake bread. So Poppo on guard. He just come in car to eat, and whoom!" Nick struck his palm with his fist. "The car hit bad."

"Hit?" Ray said.

Pete sprayed food as he yelled, "Hit by engine. We on siding like supposed to be. Engineer switching, doing saw-by. Know we there but bump us hard."

"Supper all on floor," Nick said. "Meal Poppo came to eat all over floor."

Christos said, "Poppo so mad he bust outside with his gun. We take guns from corner, follow him. All shoot engine. Then wife of foreman she stick head out from window of outfit car. Plonk! In her poor head. Nobody know who did the shoot."

"So they arrested Poppo?" I asked.

"Arrest all of us. Take us to Roseburg. But we too many for jail so they keep us in Kohlhagen Warehouse across yard tracks. Do investigation then let us go. But Roseburg people think was Poppo shoot woman. Kids on street come to him, call him names. Poppo mad now. Think Americans only ones can have good luck in this America country."

Ray said, "I wish you could all come to Santa Rosa. People there would like you."

"The meat, bread, everything was great, Christos," I said to change the subject, and stood up before Ray got to ministering.

"Eat more," Christos said and shoved a platter my way. "I'm full to burst. But thanks." I nodded to Ray and he finally stood up.

"You sleep on porch?" Nick invited.

"Thanks, but we made camp down at the river," Ray told him and scraped back his chair. "Fine meal." Pete stood too and began singing loudly in Greek, waving his arms to include us. Nick and Christos jumped up, laughing and clapping their hands, motioning us to join in. We tried to sing along, but did better at clapping and stomping. They got louder, singing faster, a lewd song to judge from the way they rolled their eyes.

"They won't miss us now," Ray said.

"Too much *ouzo*." And we clapped and stomped as we backed out the door.

22

🔵 🔵 🔵

While waiting in Roseburg we overhauled our silent horses and now we had hard work to keep them from running away with us on the good road. For several miles the way was smooth. This was too good to last long however. On top of the hills the road was filled with sharp rocks and at the foot the dust was sometimes four inches deep.

FROM THEIR LETTER TO THE *SANTA ROSA PRESS DEMOCRAT*

Next day, at the shriek of the foreman's noon whistle Ray and I set off. The postmaster remembered us. Before we could ask for it, he hauled up from under the counter our package wrapped in butcher paper. The tire was the right size, and the cyclery stood the cost, even for shipping to Oregon. After we'd collected our three dollars and promised Pete a postcard from the fair, we settled on the creek bank. I mounted the tire and Ray fussed at the bike pieces with a cloth and oilcan. I said, "By the time you're through with the overhaul, it'll be too late for a start."

"Make better time tomorrow, rested, before the heat," he agreed.

Next morning was hot soon as the sun broke over the hills, but already we were pedaling down Douglas Avenue past a line of locust trees and grand houses, one with a Buick White Streak automobile nosed into the carriage house around back.

Ray moved ahead a length, and I hollered, "You got the billiken?"

"In my blanket roll."

"Don't know why we bother." I caught up with him. He looked over at me. "'Cause he makes us smile, Vic. Far as good luck, I'd say we mostly make our own. For a Greek in this country though, it mightn't be that simple." The crunch of wheels on gravel took the place of an answer I couldn't think of.

Good roads, good tires, good spirits let the miles slip behind us, until by late afternoon we came into a lovely green valley and what must be Oakland. Brick buildings on the main street glowed deep red in the last sun, showing to advantage several fancy brass and iron door handles.

"Oakland, Oregon, is some different from Oakland, California, huh, Vic?"

We walked up to the glassed double door of Underwood Bros. Grocery. Closed. A pickle to suck on would have tasted fine, but we settled for a fill of our canteens at a pump around back. As we stood screwing the tops back on, a young fellow about our age crossed the street to us. Ray asked him, "You know of anybody looking for a couple of hands?"

The fellow gazed off, then down at his feet. "Crops are mostly in. Don't think Rochester needs anybody at the flourmill. Dr. Baker was hiring on at his gristmill last week, but I think he's full now. Best chance is up at the hop fields, Eugene way. They need help sure."

We thanked him and mounted. Just as I thought, when I turned to wave, he was standing there watching us, his head canted in a wistful manner. Through the marshy grassland north of town, the road was freshly sprinkled and fast. Took no time at all to make several more miles to where a high clearing looked proper for a fire and bedding down.

❋

"Munn, Munn," I woke myself up saying, surprised the sun already washed over the low west hills. Munn, of course, I finally remembered, was the man I lost first place to in the high jump at the track meet last year, the man from Oakland. Oakland, California, that is.

"Day's getting on." Ray tossed me a chunk of bread. "Who's Munn?"

"Nobody important," I said, scrambling to my feet.

Miles came easy this day. Mostly we skirted the rims of the valleys, where the road was higher than the grassy marshlands to either side of the invariable stream down the valley's middle. In one of the prettiest valleys yet was the little town of Yoncalla, and we stopped in front of the feed store to fill our canteens from the pump at one end of a watering trough.

"Cyclometer says six hundred eleven," I announced loud enough a couple of fellows sitting out their Sunday in chairs on the sidewalk looked over at us. "Hot day for travel," one said, then turned to watch a Ford bucket and belch its way down the street. The men laughed. "Never too hot for old man Bell," another said. "Got a jill poke fastened to the rear axle of that thing. String passed up from underneath, fastened to the steering handle. Climbs a steep hill, the motor peters out, he cuts the string. Jill poke falls, the sharp end digs in the dirt, and, whaddya know, the car doesn't go over the bank." The men laughed so hard the legs of their chairs banged down on the sidewalk boards.

We laughed with them, then I asked how the roads were to Eugene. Steep, they told us, and shook their heads. But north of town the hills weren't as bad as they'd have us believe. Or could be Ray and I were so used to walking bad roads these seemed no worse. The road followed the tracks, and we had both to ourselves for some miles.

Coming on the burned-out remains of a fine resort hotel, we decided to have a look around, see if we could find the hot springs, the usual California reason for a big hotel. Sure enough, at a low concrete encasement, steam rose from a split in the wood covering.

"Sulphur springs all right." Holding my nose then I talked in a twang. "Cures blood disorders, rheumatism, stomach trouble, kidney disease, poison oak, sore throat, and flat feet," I rattled off like a side-show spieler. "One half glass before each meal. If this doesn't work, try drinking what's in the glass. If that doesn't work, throw it up, you're sure to feel better." I made coarse retching sounds. Ray laughed till he had to catch his breath, and I wished I could think of more so we'd have a long howl together.

From there it was push and walk because of the ankle-deep dust. Tired enough, hungry enough, we made camp on the north side of the little town of Drain.

Next morning was warm even at seven, but we made Cottage Grove by early afternoon. And even better time nearly to Springfield, where we made camp on the bank of a fork of the Willamette River, a walloping lot of water. Ray was already fishing when I spotted a sign nailed to a tree near the road and walked closer to read it: 'Hop pickers wanted. Next road to left.'

23

❀ ❀ ❀

Dear Mama, I am still well. My hand is alright now. It wasn't bad...
I haven't been a bit homesick. I don't have time, too much
happening. Lots of nice people in Oregon, and they give us
vegetables and fruit. Sorry to hear you are losing weight. I
wonder if you worry about me. Your son, Victor.

FROM A PENNY POSTCARD

Next day we asked for work at the Snowball Flour Mill in
Springfield, but were turned away. The Booth-Kelly Lumber
Mill just out of town gave us the same answer. By the time
we headed down the dusty road to the hop yard it was coming on
evening. Two hop barns were boxy silhouettes against the western
sky, the chimneys on each roof poking up like outhouses.

Ray cocked his head. "Music?"

"Sounds like." My skin prickled. Music outside on a warm
evening spelled people and good times. Tents were pitched under
the trees on both sides, and down the road ahead of us, women,
men, and youngsters laughed and talked as they jollied their way
toward the music. Sure enough, on a raised platform out in a field,
couples bobbed and bounced to the rhythm of a fiddle and
accordion playing a schottische. Gathered around, folks smiled at
the dancers and tapped their feet, while little children darted in and
out of the clumps of skirts and trousers. Off a ways a bonfire leaped
to life as several young men threw on logs.

Our wheels secured to a tether stake, we joined the folks ambling
toward the platform, just as a lovely girl with heavy dark hair in a
coil at the back of her neck climbed the platform steps and began to
dance with a younger girl.

"She's got eyes for you," Ray whispered.

"Who?"

"The pretty one with the dark hair."

"Nah." But then the music stopped, and the girl sure enough looked over, right at me.

"You fellows new at picking?" Another girl was at Ray's side. About our age, she had little brown curls all around her face and wore a blue dress with a big white collar.

"We hope to get on tomorrow," he told her. The music started up again. She flashed him a smile, inclined her head toward the musicians and motioned for him to move with her away from the platform. I stayed put. If I left, I might never see the dark-haired girl again. I searched for her now among the growing number of waltzing couples, all looking anything but tired after a day in the fields. Then, and yes, glancing over at me, down the steps she came with the younger girl. Now she spoke to a woman who took the youngster by the hand and they mounted the steps.

My gaze wouldn't leave the girl, beautiful in a dark skirt that brushed her ankles and a white waist with frills at the neck. She saw me watching her and lowered her eyes. I forced myself to look at the dancers. When I glanced back, the girl had stepped nearer me. Before I knew what I was about, I was beside her asking her to dance. "I'd like to." Her voice was soft. The music started up: "Jimmy-Crack-Corn and I Don't Care." The fiddle took off under full steam. The accordion jumped in, igniting the dancers.

"Could we wait for a waltz?" I asked her. "That's about all I know how to do."

"Then let's go sit by the fire." Her eyes looked to be hazel or maybe green, deep-set and full of so much I'd never know. And this beauty wanted to sit by me. We walked side by side, her skirt rippling, her splendid hair shining in the last of twilight. How I wished I'd put on my other shirt and stopped to wash off the dust.

She seemed smaller as we sat on the log, the firelight playing its own dance about the smooth planes of her cheeks and forehead. On the other side of the roaring blaze, among folks on the logs opposite, sat Ray and the girl with the white collar. I hoped he might leave off gazing at her long enough to see me beside my own beautiful girl, but he was full taken.

"My name is Rose," she was saying.

"Vic McDaniel." Could she see my heart thumping like a donkey engine?

"Rose Hampton. My father is weigh master. During hop season, that is." She smiled the most beguiling smile, her teeth even and white, eyes lively. "The rest of the year he teaches chemistry at the University in Eugene."

"A professor? Don't think I ever knew a professor. He the one my friend and I should talk to about getting on tomorrow?" She laughed, and it was like the lilt of a stream in the quiet of night after you'd rolled up. "Papa's same as anybody else. Mr. Sumner is usually the one you'd talk to, but he'll be gone tomorrow, so Papa could hire you. I'm sure he will."

As we talked, the ring of people around the fire grew until the seats were filled and folks stood behind them. I told Rose about the miles we'd come and our hope to see the Alaska-Yukon-Pacific Exposition in Seattle, and about the Forestry Building that was held up by great logs forty feet high. I didn't say about the Igorot puppy eaters or the hula dancers. She tipped her head, listening, those lovely girl-eyes on me alone. Then she told me about her grandfather who came out on the Oregon Trail. "No hops here when Grandpa arrived." She laughed her sweet-flowing laugh, and the heat surged through me.

"Wasn't much but Indians and nice country, I'd venture," I said, shifting.

"That's right. But Papa says if more Oregon counties go prohibition, soon there'll be no hops again. Says then Oregon will have only flax and mint for money crops. But Mr. Sumner sells most of his bales to the German breweries in Portland and Vancouver, Washington. Be awhile before they go prohibition, Papa says." Rose was as nervous as I was, talking about all these things that didn't matter. But I hoped she wouldn't stop. I craved to watch the little crinkles come in her forehead, and the way her full lips curved around her words to make each one sound like ripe fruit.

"So, would you like to stay?"

"Stay?" What had I missed?

"The man with the mouth organ. He just asked if folks want to stay and sing. So do you want to?" Before I could answer, Rose turned quickly. Her mother and sister had come from behind, and Rose got up. "I have to go now. Maybe I'll see you in the fields tomorrow." I pulled to my feet, feeling suddenly hollow and desperate for her to stay. But I said, "Hope so," then nodded to her mother and tipped my cap. "Ma'am."

Rose said, "No picking until ten. After the vines are dry. They don't want to pay us for the night's dew on the hop flowers." She laughed water music.

By eight o'clock next morning Ray and I had chained the bikes at one of the platform posts and walked between rows of poles. At rows' end, a tall man stood next to a scales and overhead hook as he wrote intently on a tablet.

"Slow now, Blackie," came an old man's voice from two rows up. There a slight fellow astride a pony stood in the stirrups to reach the poles where he was stringing twine. "Pretty smart," I said to Ray, recalling Uncle Ben's fields and how we used to clamber up and down ladders, dragging them from pole to pole to do what this codger did from his pony.

" 'Morning," called the man at the scales.

" 'Morning, sir," we chorused.

"You lads wanting to hire on?"

"Yes, sir," I said, reaching him. "Would you be Mr. Hampton?"

"I would. We need a couple of young bucks to load sacks in the wagon after I weigh them." He pointed to a spring wagon next to the nearest hop barn. "You understand this business?"

Ray said, "We picked back home."

I was disappointed not to work in the fields alongside Rose, but that was not to be. I could only hope I might see her, maybe pass some words.

"Pickers won't start for some while," Mr. Hampton said. "Then, takes time to fill their baskets, empty them in the sacks, and for me or for you to weigh them. You want to do odd jobs till then?"

"Yes, sir," we said.

He started toward the near barn, then stopped and hollered to the old man on the pony, "Tell Timmy he's high pole man today." To us, "Women have trouble reaching the higher vines. Need a ladder man to come pull them down." He pointed ahead. "That pile of wood. Stack it in the barns for the sulphur fires. When the wood's in, grab a fork and start turning the hops on the bottom floor racks, this barn first. If there's time, the second floor. A dollar a day. Pickers have to bring in a hundred pounds for that."

We told him the pay was fine and started for the woodpile. In Santa Rosa pickers got a penny a pound too. All I ever was able to bring in was eighty or ninety pounds. But now I'd forfeit my dollar just to spend the day with Rose.

At twelve o'clock Mr. Hampton blew the whistle for lunch. Ray and I rounded the barn, having not quite finished turning the twenty-inch-deep rack of half-cured hops on the lower floor of the second barn. Pickers were gathering, meeting one another at the end of the rows. Women dug under the vines where they had stashed cloth-tied bundles of food and yelled at the kids hiding there to come out and eat.

"Vic?" Rose's voice behind us. "I made sandwiches enough for you. And Beth made some for Ray." I turned. There they were, half-skipping to catch up to us. Ray's girl and Rose in wide-brimmed hats and long-sleeved dusters, Beth's green, Rose's dark blue.

Rose scooted past us to lead the way, calling over her shoulder, "Come on." Beth followed, with Ray and me at their heels, our smiles wide as wagon beds. Under a large pine, we ate boiled eggs, peaches, and thick roast beef sandwiches. "Tell us about your trip." Rose looked full into my face, her large eyes definitely hazel. "Beth and I have been to Salem. But Seattle is so far away. And I'd be afraid ever to go to California, for the earthquakes." The girls looked at each other and shivered.

When Ray started to answer, I worried he might describe the big quake, tell how Santa Rosa had more deaths for its size than San Francisco, or that folks still woke up at night screaming. Better the girls should hear about us. Ray talked about us all right, and it was no minister's voice he used either, even tugging at the truth here and there to make the story better, about the forest fire, and my tumble off the mountain. I jumped in there, because the girls wanted to look at my wound. Rose even ran her finger along the red jag on my palm, sending flash lightning clean to my spine. I told them a man has to expect to get hurt on a trip as long as ours, that you learn not to pay any mind to pains or you'll never get to where you're going. Mr. Hampton's whistle came too soon.

"We'll be at the campfire tonight," Rose said, and Beth nodded, as we all got up from the grass. The girls stuffed what we hadn't eaten in a bandanna. For some queer reason the yellow-jackets paid no heed either to them or the food, while Ray and I swung our caps about our legs and feet to keep the pesky things from settling on the hop juice we'd collected.

When we'd said our thanks for the eats, I finished, "We'll see you at the campfire." I tried to think of a reason then to run over to the near kiln and climb the rope used to lower the bales that hung from the second floor door. At Uncle Ben's I was the only one could go up the two-story rope hand over hand. But a reason never came.

The afternoon was long. Ray and I worked fast, and as well as we knew how, each of us too full of thoughts to be tired. Mr. Hampton must have been pleased enough. When he checked us out, he said, "Eight o'clock tomorrow. Only a half day. Pickers quit at noon. Barns will be full by then."

Later, in the river next to camp, we soaped off while the fire settled, and a certain foolishness took me. I hollered, "If you're gonna marry Beth, you're gonna have to feed her persimmons so her face goes sour. Preacher's not supposed to have a pretty wife." I gave him a shove and he plopped backwards spluttering. "So how long you s'pose it's gonna take Rose to teach you manners enough to sit at the same table with a father-in-law professor, huh?" He reared up and cuffed me, knocking the soap downstream so I had to dive after it.

But at the campfire, sitting on the logs waiting for the girls, the colt in us had died. Maybe they wouldn't come. The thought eased my stomach some, but sent a coldness from my belly both ways. If they didn't come, I'd never sleep tonight for the torment. But if they did. . . . Music from the platform now was soft and drowsy, "Bring Back My Bonnie." A half dozen or so couples moved slowly to the lazy strains. Beside me, Ray opened the newspaper one of the fire-starter fellows had given him, the *Eugene Register Guard*. He lowered it to read by the light of the fire, as though the paper were important. "Lane County Fair has mud wrestling and a man who plays two cornets at once," he mumbled.

I first recognized Rose's little sister and her mother. Behind them, yes, Rose and Beth, Rose in a waist, this one plain, with no frills at the throat. My knees felt like noodles when I stood up. Her mother barely nodded. "Half an hour," she said to the girls as they sat beside us. I was relieved she took the little sister with her.

Ray said to Beth, "Move across?"

"Papa said you work hard," Rose began after Ray and Beth found places on the log opposite.

"Hmm. Bet the university students like him. He's a good explainer. About hops anyway."

She smiled, but shyer than before. I remembered her rightly, the perfect teeth, how her dark hair came loose in small, soft strands over her ears. "Yes," she said, seeming to want to say more. Then facing me, "Vic, do you know anything about a rabbit on the second floor drying rack?" "Rabbit? Running around the kiln drying rack?" The fire flared, and the women on the side log screamed. Two jumped up, but sat back down when the blaze quieted.

"Not running, silly." The tiny furrows came in Rose's lovely brow. "Papa said Mr. Grubbe found the rabbit when he made his rounds. It was dead, killed by a clod likely. Over in one corner.

Hops around it were already near ruined. Doesn't take long in hot weather. A whole floor can spoil in a half day. Folks, kids mostly, put anything they can find in their sack to get more weight. Especially if they think they can flam the weigh master, or some new loader. I told Papa it couldn't have been you boys, but he said you were loading near the weigh station. Said you could have seen the hooligan, maybe even helped. Anyway, he said you were the last ones up on the second floor. If it wasn't you did it, you should have found the rabbit and told him." Rose's eyes had turned to coal. "It wasn't you, was it?"

"Rose, 'course it wasn't us. We're not the sort that's out for devilment. We wouldn't do harm apurpose, ever."

"I knew it wasn't. But Papa says he'll see you load from the baler tomorrow. That's the hardest job of all." Tears spilled down her cheeks, but she wiped them quickly when she saw her mother and sister come into the circle of firelight. My soul was sick. "Rose. Please, Rose." I wanted to take her hand but was afraid. Then, in a startle, I heard myself burst out, "S'pose you and Beth could go to the fair? To Eugene? With Ray and me tomorrow afternoon?"

She almost smiled as she stood to go, so beautiful in the flickering light. "No, Vic," was all she said, and moved to her mother and sister. Beth was by her side, the girls taking each others' arms. Neither looked back at Ray, now at my side, or me. In the instant, they were absorbed by the inky black, it dousing the rich warm light that had burned inside me.

"No moon tonight," Ray said, his voice cracking.

"'Course not. I'll be surprised if the sun comes up tomorrow."

"All because of a damned rabbit." I couldn't remember Ray swearing but a few times since we were in third grade. Only when he had to, like now.

24

∰ ∰ ∰

We pushed on to the town of Eugene and were surprised to
find such a lively little city. As we glided along the well-paved
streets, the handsome buildings of the University and many
beautiful residences were passed. . . . The county fair is now
being held here.

FROM THEIR LETTER TO THE *SANTA ROSA PRESS DEMOCRAT*

Afternoon saw us thumping over the wide planks of the long
bridge across the river from Springfield to Eugene City. The
sun warm on my back couldn't take the chill off my
disposition, and the tidy three dollars in our pockets didn't quiet my
churning. I ached to square ourselves with Professor Hampton.
Because of a clod-pated rabbit our chances with Beth and Rose had
gone to smithereens. I pounded a fist on the handlebar.

Ray swiveled and yelled, "Right here used to be the longest
covered bridge in the state. Flood took it out in '81, newspaper
said." Nothing on his mind that a good fact wouldn't cure, and I
pounded the handlebar again.

We hadn't seen Hampton at the yards that morning. Timmy, the
high-poler, met us at the weigh station, told us the professor said we
should unload from the baler. Rose was right; the work was heavy,
though nothing to compare with the load of not being able to
defend ourselves against Hampton's charge.

Off the bridge now, our tires skimmed Eugene City's newly
paved streets. We stopped at the grand Commercial Club building
where we picked up a pamphlet called *Anybody's Magazine* and sat
on the front steps to read about the fair. River rat stunts were going
on right now. A magic man, Zolsto, performed in a special tent in
the fairgrounds across from the courthouse. A fat lady flirted in the
Tent of Wonders. Mud wrestling was scheduled for five o'clock. Ray
stuffed the paper in his pocket and we mounted up.

"So, you want to go?" I hollered over the barking of two good-
sized dogs chasing us. Over his shoulder he yelled, "I don't have the

spirit." "Me too," I shouted, though the dogs had peeled off to bark at a horse and dung cart.

Across from the handsome brick courthouse crowds milled among many tents. A spieler called raspy-voiced about a girl inside who had been asleep for twenty years and you could come in and see her for two-bits.

"Without that rabbit we'd have had the heart to at least see the mud wrestling," I said, riding alongside.

"Want to change our minds?"

"I just want to get out of town, make camp early. You?"

"Yeah." We stopped at a pie wagon with big slanted letters on the side: *Skinner's Mudhole*. In the bandstand nearby, a band played "Two Little Girls in Blue." We had two pieces of apple pie each, while I listened to the music and missed Rose. Fresh money in our purse, we ordered four more pieces of the peach pie for later. Nearly out of town and my stomach with no hollows, Ray informed, "Skinner's Mudhole, that's what folks used to call Eugene City. After Eugene Skinner, paper said." Ray was so pleased with himself he chuckled. In an easy pedal down the street out of town, I stayed quiet. All this friend of mine needed to settle a nasty score inside himself was to parade a shiny, new fact. It made me wonder.

Before the bridge north, we made camp on the river bank a short ways from a dock where two sternwheelers were tied up. Smoke plumed from the stack of the *Grey Eagle*, the boat nearest. Next to her, *The City of Eugene's* stack was cold. Next morning I came awake to the throb of *The City of Eugene's* steam engine, and scrambled to my feet. By the time I was cinching my roll to the bike a wagon bumped down the steep bank road onto the boat's loading ramp, but we decided not to wait till she was underway.

"Grab your pie, Vic. Let's head to the bridge across the millrace."

As we crossed the narrow plank bridge over the tree-lined channel of water, the stern end of a canoe was just slipping silently beneath the spread of a willow on the west bank to disappear in the thick growth. Then, out from there came the burble of a young woman's laugh. Oh, how I missed Rose.

On the lane Ray pedaled a few lengths ahead. "Sign," he hollered. Barely readable on a weathered board nailed to a cedar was: Junction City, with an arrow, and we turned north. Once out of town the road followed the rails through this marshy, skillet-flat land, and was as dusty as any we'd hit since Shasta Springs.

Villard Hall, State University, Eugene, Ore.

Suddenly, off to the right in a great thrashing of wings and beating of air, a mass of large water birds lifted up, squawking like an army of rusted hens, all but darkening the sky. My breath stopped from the wonder of them. Then more birds by the legion rose from the brown-red marsh grass, seemed like an acre at a time, each clot of them lifting and wheeling as a single body. They were geese right enough, heavy-bodied getting off the ground, but once up flying with a weightless grace and precision to join the others and form a majestic cloud that circled once, twice, a great galaxy up there. As one they descended then, gliding lower, and lower still, hovering, to settle finally some distance off and sink from view, except for the few milling, gabbling souls in search of a particular place to put down in that ocean of geese. At once it was as if they had never been, the afternoon sky an uncluttered blue, the phalanx of thunderheads resting their bellies on the Cascade Mountains, and the only sound and movement the tall grass riffling and rustling in the small breeze.

Astride the wheels, we just looked at each other. "Must have been a thousand," I whispered, feeling as though I'd been to church. "More," he breathed. "Marshes and grain they go together like a soft bed and a full meal." North through fields of barley, oats and wheat, a few scattered flocks of birds, ducks, a few cranes, lifted and landed, but we saw no more geese.

At Junction City we stopped to fill our canteens at a pump around the corner from O. Peterson's Blacksmithing and talked to several Scandinavian farmers, one about to buy a cream separator. They said crops in these parts were as fine as any in the world. We told them about the great California valley, but they looked skeptical. After spending more than a dollar on some apples and milk and bread, we leaned against a trough and watched the steady parade of farm wagons and drays.

By the time we neared Harrisburg, twilight was lowering. The posted sign on the riverbank told us what we'd already surmised: the day's last crossing had been a full hour earlier. Now the raft-like ferry was tied up on the opposite bank, its dinghy tethered to its side. Both bobbed gently in the current just upstream of several riverfront buildings built on pilings and with loading platforms.

We got startled awake that night, seemed like right after we dropped off; a light sprinkle damped my face and made whispery sounds in the grass all about. While I was figuring it out, the sprinkle turned heavy. Ray had rolled up under the near willows and yelled, "You'll pack a wet blanket if you don't move." I found a dry spot under a farther tree, on a steep slant, but I was too sleepy to care.

Next morning, soon as the ferry put its ramp down on our side, we were pushing onto it. The ride cost fifteen cents each, same as for a man and his animal. Shortly, a couple of crease-faced farmers drove their teams and wagons loaded with grain sacks down the bank road and up the ramp, all but filling the boat that looked more like a barge with side rails and ramps at both ends.

When the wagon drivers had feed bags on their animals they joined Ray and me near the ferryman and his wheel. A small boy in a hat too big sat on an upended bucket and watched each of us, then settled his gaze on the ferryman who was likely his pa. The ferryman turned the big wheel a quarter turn. A pulley on one of the ropes running to the overhead lines screeched, then quieted, and the ferry canted into the current. "Yessir, fine year for the river," the ferryman said. "Plenty of water. Boats get clear up to Eugene, even this late. Many a year water gives out. Only flat-bottoms get through."

"What's this?" the boy piped. I hadn't seen him move to our bikes leaning against the rail. Crouched over my Veeder, he rubbed the nickel barrel clean. "There's numbers."

"They tell how far we've come," I said, moving beside him. "My friend and I have biked, let's see." I peered around the boy's big hat. "Says we've traveled seven hundred and two miles."

"You from New York?" The youngster stood up to get a better look at Ray and me.

"Santa Rosa, California," Ray answered. "On our way to the Alaska-Pacific-Yukon-Exposition in Seattle." Silenced, the boy moved from the bicycles to stand next to his father, who now turned the wheel the smallest bit. The boat groaned to shore, water slapping the bank ahead of it. Quitting the wheel, the ferryman strode forward and loosed the rope to lower the ramp. The farmers heisted up to their wagon seats.

Out of town the road was hard-packed and straight as a rod. Miles streaked behind us through the grain fields and scattered small farms, some with dairy herds. By afternoon, the peaks of the Cascades showed themselves, remote, tipped rosy-white in the sunset light.

Tired as we were, we had to have a swing through the city of Albany, down Ferry Street to the big bridge, and on Lyon Street we followed an electric trolley that looked spanking new.

The road out of town dipped and swelled, more to be felt than seen now that night had fallen, and it too quickly. Crossing the Santiam Bridge, the water down there looked forbidding, dark and heavy as flowing sorghum. Ray had pedaled beyond range of my headlamp, and a panic gripped me. I blew my whistle. His bell answered. At last on the north side of the river I yelled, "We shouldn't travel on into night like this," and was embarrassed at the struggle in my voice.

When we'd found a level place to put down, I wheeled in front of his lamp and bent over the cyclometer. "Thirty-seven miles under us today," and hoped I sounded my natural, unafraid self. "Not worth travel in the dark though, Vic." For sure I would be in Ray's prayers tonight, and the thought was a discomfort.

25

❀ ❀ ❀

On account of the poor roads we did not reach Salem until afternoon. . . . Visited the state capitol. . . rode on to the fair grounds, which are two miles from the city. . . . Among the stock exhibits we saw herds of cattle from California.

FROM THEIR LETTER TO THE *SANTA ROSA PRESS DEMOCRAT*

The sun barely two hands above the Cascades saw us pedaling through the little town of Jefferson, where a few men hurried along the dusty main street in the direction of the mill, lard buckets swinging at their sides. "Mornin'," they'd say, but I fancied they had their opinions about two lunks pleasuring around on bicycles instead of working like respectable folks.

Just outside town we hit corduroy. Logs were whole in places, but rotted out in more. We got off and walked, bikes bouncing along as we avoided the rot holes, some big as milk cans. North of a little hamlet called Marion, Ray stopped at a crest and leaned on the handlebars to puzzle out the road ahead. "Looks like planks," he said as I pulled up. Sure enough, the road was thick dust over wide boards fixed close together. It was slow but level; we stayed mounted. "Planks must put a spook in the teams come winter." Ray's words thudded to the pound of his wheels on the boards. I said, "Dust turned to fulsome mud would grease these planks like a griddle. Bring a horse down in a mighty hurry."

Soon our miles were mostly on foot. This low land was given to planked roads, and beneath the dust, too often rotten. After crossing a shallow creek where the bridge was out, we stood aside for a stage coming up fast. The span never broke gait through the water and out. Churning past, animals and wheels shot mud and water all ways. The driver yelled, "Sorry men. Making up time." Hours later, after puffing up a long grade, we stopped at the summit. In front of us, couched in soft, rolling country, lay the city of Salem, its streets heavy with trees.

We rode straight to the Capitol building, which was more than grand. Its copper dome shone like a fresh-minted Lincoln penny high above the Greek-columned entry. Worlds larger than Santa Rosa's courthouse, the big one built after the quake, this was, after all, the capitol building for a state. Folks didn't seem to mind walking around us as we stood there gawking, appreciating their fine capitol.

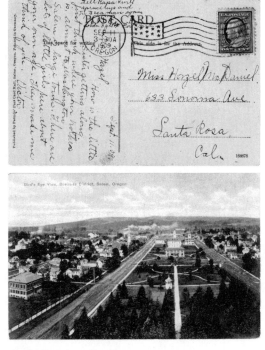

Ray said, "Salem had itself a big do last February. That's when Oregon was fifty years a state."

"You hear about it at home?"

"In the paper," he said. I imagined he was disappointed I could never talk with him about what he knew from his readings, so I didn't ask more about the big do, though I would have liked to.

By the time we made it out to their fairgrounds it was coming on twilight, too dark to see much. At the office we learned the fair was about to close anyway, but the man said we'd still have time for a quick look at the stock exhibits. In the splendid barns we pushed our wheels along in the sawdust between row after row of scrubbed, well-conformed cattle. A sign in front of the last barn bragged that inside was an exhibit herd from California, so we had to give a look. The animals favored all the others, far as we could tell, but now we'd have a true morsel for the paper.

Outside was close to dark, but the road let us stay mounted for the four miles to a creek near Brooks where oak trees gave shelter enough to bed down.

✦

I sniffed something bittery as I came awake next morning and yelled, "You smell hop flowers?" Ray squatted by the fire and flipped the sticks that held breakfast. "Likely left over from those dreams you couldn't let loose of, 'bout Rose maybe? And hops." His chin was tacked to his chest to hide his for-sure smile. "Got a few dreams of your own, I wager." It ruffled me he could see into my thoughts, but now he probed at my dreams.

Less than half an hour later saw us pedaling north. Out of Brooks, able to stay mounted on the side verge, I yahooed, "Ex-po-si-tion!" Behind me Ray belted, "I'll—meet—you—in—Se—attle," coming close to the tune of the song that started out that way.

"Want to take in the dancers at that Oriental Village on the Pay Streak?" A chuckhole put emphasis on my "Pay." I added, "Girls come near to wearing nothing at all, I heard." "Sure," Ray agreed. "But we'll write Santa Rosa about walking along the Gay Way, and the rides on the Tickler or the Joy Wheel or the Vacuum Tube, say how we saw the battle of the *Merrimac* and the *Monitor* and came out holding our ears from the canons and coughing from the smoke." "You're a trusty chum, Ray," I hollered, filled with the knowing of it.

In Hubbard, a few houses and a store, we bought two roast beef sandwiches from the wife of the keeper. She took our twenty cents and moved to the onion barrel to help a little girl pick out two sweet onions. We stood at the counter dividing our remaining money and sniffing the tidy odor of freshly-oiled floor boards. Ray said, "Don't see many of these anymore," and dropped the three dollar gold piece in his purse, plunking after it the two two-bit pieces and two dimes a coin at a time. I stuffed the three silver dollars and the seventy-five cents down my rucksack, as though I were used to carrying money any which place.

I had suggested the split earlier. "Portland's a big place," I told him. "If we get separated, we should each of us have money." But in a cranny of my mind lived the hope that in Portland, while Ray busied himself oiling the bikes, I might just take a look at what an open town could offer. I saw mention in Eugene City's *Anybody's Magazine* of Portland's more than five hundred saloons, one of them sporting the longest bar in the world, in the shape of a horseshoe. Now with the extra nickel over our halves in my sack, I might just buy myself a drink of their beer at that horseshoe bar and taste what Oregon hops could do.

Back on the wheels, we picked up speed at the edge of town on a road lately graded. Passing a vast hop field, I suffered the stab of my loss of sweet Rose. Truth be known, as more time and distance was put between us, the greater her sweetness became, until Rose now seemed like the girl I had waited for these long years, and I wondered if I might be in love.

At Oregon City we stopped at the town park that appeared to be the grounds of a fine house. A heavy woman with her gray hair pulled back in a tight bun like my Aunt Nora's came up to us and said we looked the age of her grandsons. When we asked about the fine house, she told us a Dr. McLoughlin built it in 1845. "The father of Oregon," she told us. "Used to be the Pacific Coast head of the Hudson's Bay Company." Her bright blue eyes sparkled, and I saw my Aunt Nora. We thanked her and told her we hoped her grandsons came to visit often.

Just north of town we had a choice of roads heading to Portland. The west road crossed a suspension bridge, then appeared to follow the river, now a whopping lot wider and more powerful than when we first met it farther south. Until the town of Oswego we were pleased with our choice. We could stay mounted, and the river was broad enough for interesting traffic: good-sized workboats and barges, a procession of skiffs and dories. But after a rail crossing and bridge, we left the river. In dust nearly to our calves we dismounted. The road took off sharply up a steep, narrow grade through dense timber.

"Think we should roll up? Take the grade tomorrow?" I asked. The sun had slipped behind the hills.

"Same grade's going to be there in the morning, Vic."

Through dust puppy-deep, between black walls of trees, we pushed up the steep incline that sharpened near the summit to maybe fifteen percent. Panting and puffing, we plodded between the ruts. Sweat beaded my forehead even in the cool air; our wheels were heavy and balky in the mattress of dust. At last, glad for the crest, we stopped and found our breath.

We'd hoped for our first look at the lay of the big city, but near hills were too much in the way. Still, in the distance, against the green-gray of lowering dusk and above the dark, forested horizon, more than a few buildings picked up the last of the sun's rays very near the winding glint of a far river. "Portland," we murmured together.

26

🌀 🌀 🌀

Dear Papa and Mama:

Received Papa's card tonight. We're now seeing Portland. Say but it's great. I shall never forget this trip. I am seeing more of the world every day. Your son, Victor

FROM A PENNY POSTCARD

We coasted lickety-split down the graveled, winding grade, the cool air freshening us, along with our spirits. More and more lights pricked on, though the west sky still blazed reds and oranges.

"Bigger than I thought," Ray yelled back, an excitement in his voice. "And there's our Willamette River, all grown up. Runs right—through—town." A rock stumbled his talk, as he took a hand from the bars to sweep it north, where in the distance another river flowed hugely east to west. "And there, the absolute—ly, true Co—lumbia River."

A mighty swath of water it was too, the broad path of it catching the low light along its massive passage to the sea. "Lewis and Clark and their boys must have had themselves a fine sail down that old river," I hollered, while it struck me they could have felt the same inside tingles at their first sight of this country as Ray and I did now, a hundred years later.

Soon we would be in Portland. I realized suddenly that the tiredness which had ached my every bone on the other side of the hill had stayed there—on the other side of the hill; I felt brand new. "Look there." I waved east where Mt. Hood rose in a snowy cone that sunset had turned to strawberry cream. Less than ten minutes later we pedaled along a paved street smack in the hubbub of an honest-to-Sam city.

Already we had met three automobiles and passed several more. Drays, express wagons, one-horse deliveries, buggies added to the

muddle even at this hour on Monday. Pedestrians, mostly men in
dark suits and bowlers, walked with important steps in front of us,
behind us, off and on the street, swarming the sidewalks thick as
flies on a flop. To each side, cheek-by-jowl buildings towered eight
to ten stories, and were fancily decorated with arched entries and
heavy doors that held thick, figured glass, and facades ringed round
with fierce-looking lions or sturdy ladies wearing spiked crowns.

"Watch out, Vic! You near ran down that fellow and his trash
cart."

We bounced over electric car tracks, and threaded through the
wagons and walkers, my pulse at full gallop. I wanted to holler and
shout, be part of the noise. Ahead, a streetcar clanged and started
up. Horses whinnied and snorted as they clopped along on the
macadam. Everywhere, the clatter of wheel rims. Off a ways a horn
oog-aahed. Not since I was in San Francisco when I was ten had I
seen and heard a city, and I was too young then to feel the throb
and beat of thousands of folks living close.

"Find a park where we can roll up?" Ray yelled.

"Down this street looks like the courthouse." We signaled our
arms for a left turn.

The government buildings' grounds were wide-reaching, with
bushes and trees enough we could disappear from scrutiny. And the
Post Office was bound to be nearby. Later, as we lay rolled up under
a rhododendron the size of a wood shed, our blankets back to back,
my every muscle had its own story about how long our day had
been. Even the street noise wouldn't steal my sleep this night.
"Cyclometer says eight hundred and ten," I said, my eyes shutting
down.

Ray muttered, "Tomorrow, have to find Burnside Street. See that
longest bar in the world," and grunted.

Tomorrow came quick enough. A dinging streetcar bell brought
me awake. My blanket felt clammy from the fog that veiled the
whole world and dripped from the trees like rain. Ray was packed
and chewing jerky as he sat on the grass watching a Metropolitan
electric car unload then load flocks of people, the action looking
staged behind a gray scrim. Conductors at either end of the car, at
the tiller and the back door, stood smartly erect in their double-
breasted dark uniforms and squared-off caps. The people scrambling
on and off looked only in a hurry.

Once packed, I grabbed some jerky, and puzzled if the odd
wonder in me was born of the leavings from a last night's dream, or

if Ray really had suggested we go see that longest bar. If he had, was it just sleep talk? Either way, I decided not to ask him.

Locking our wheels in front of the courthouse seemed as safe a place as we might find. Free of the bikes, we could see the city. A sling of our rucksacks on our backs and we were off. Fog seemed even denser, but a man at the foot of the courthouse steps told us it was sure to lift by noon. At the Post Office we headed for the General Delivery window where I had a fine letter from little Hazel, and one from Papa and Mama. A note from Finley said town folks liked what we wrote and to keep sending our letters. Ray's mother wrote how she and his sister missed him and asking when did he think he could come home. She sent a money order for five dollars, which he cashed right there in the Post Office.

"Now we shouldn't have to work again before Seattle," he said.

"But your mama wants you to get home on that money. We sure won't spend it 'less we have to."

Electric car after car took us from one end of the great city to the other. I couldn't remember when the fog disappeared, but the sun was a warm one all afternoon. We got off at the police headquarters because the conductor said prisoners from the basement jail were let out in the daytime to work in the shops up and down the street. In a small grocery we bought some bread and cheese, then shuffled about in a big market with marble-countered stalls, but we never saw anyone who looked like a let-out criminal.

It was some after the sun sank that the conductor called, "Burnside." On the instant Ray and I both reached up to pull the cord. From where we got off it wasn't far to the building with the small oval sign: Erickson's Saloon.

"There's still light. You want to go back? Clean the bikes?" I watched him closely. Yes I wanted to see that bar; what I wasn't sure I wanted was to see Ray in a saloon. "Plenty of time to bike-clean in Washington where the bars aren't as long, Vic." Ray definitely had not been sleep-talking last night. I grinned. But this friend of mine best get all his parts going the same direction if he's thinking to one day march down that narrow churchy aisle with a band around his collar, was my feel for it.

Erickson's was as much arena as saloon. More men filled the place than I'd ever seen in a single room. Crowded around tables, standing at the back and side walls along what must have been the bar, milling, talking in groups as they entered behind us, laughing and slapping each other on the back. The air was blue smoke that drifted in lazy clouds about the lamps dangling on long cords from the high ceiling. Every man wore either a pipe or cigar in his mouth, taking it out only to talk or drink. From somewhere down at the end of the room waves of laughter and banjo music pulsed through the vast assembly of hatted, smoking, card-playing drinkers and talkers.

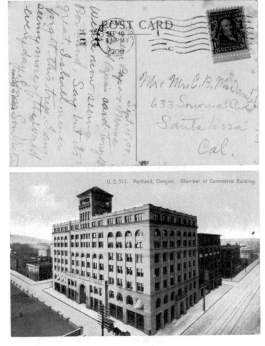

U. S. 515.   Portland, Oregon.   Chamber of Commerce Building.

"You boys meeting someone?" A short man in a wrinkled gray suit crowded close.

"Just here to look," I yelled over the din.

"There's a store of lookin' to be done, lads." The fellow had Ray and me by the elbows. "This way," he hollered in a friendly way and guided us between several groups to a round table where a white-bearded fellow leaned back in his chair and stared into his glass. "Sit down, m'lads," said our chummy fellow. "You need a drink. It's a fearsome wait at the bar. I'll just mosey around, tell Charlie we got newcomers needs good treatment."

"No cause you should trouble for us," Ray said. I said, "We'll buy our own, and thanks." I slipped off my pack, set it on the table and dug out the money.

"We're a city likes to show folks a good time. Now you boys look around. I'll be back with a couple of Oregon beers and wait for you."

"All right." I slapped two nickels in his hand. "We'll just look about. Meet you back here."

Off from the main room were other rooms, one with private booths behind large wooden panels. Men carrying drinks moved from place to place. A large sign on the wall listed a number of locations in the building that honored Erickson's checks, whatever they might be. A barbershop, the back room, a bootblack stand. Ray talked near my ear. "A man could live right here and never need to leave."

To judge from the mob that crowded three and four deep down the length of one long wall and curved into another, and then another, the bar was for sure a far-going one. We edged closer. Then, through the jostling mob, we saw the bar: a thick slab of handsome dark wood polished like a mirror.

"Better muscle in if you want a drink," a tall fellow shouted next to us. His fedora pulled low over one eye gave him the look of a dandy, but his angular, stubbled face looked down at us openly. "We have a drink waiting at a table," Ray told him. "We're mostly interested in seeing that bar. The longest in the world?"

"That's right. When the town was under water during the big flood in '89, the boys tell they couldn't be parted from that bar. Just took it up so's it'd float, and had their drinks as usual. I think I believe it, though beer spins some fine yarns." The fellow had a deep laugh that rumbled through his spare frame. "Name's Amos. You men from around here?" He held out a hand, and we shook.

"Come down to the end here where we can talk and you can appreciate the beauty of the wood in this bar." He gestured to where several stools stood empty.

"On our way to Seattle to see the fair," Ray offered, as we slid our hands over the bar's velvet-smooth surface.

"Fine fair. Friend of mine just got back. Says it's as good as ours was in aught five, lots of it almost the same, he said. For ten cents you can get a ride on Lake Washington. Grandest body of fresh water west of the Great Lakes, they like to call it. My friend says that may even be true."

Amos motioned us to sit on the stools, taking some care to flip out his coat tails before perching between us. His were not the clothes of a laboring man. "I want to tell you boys the gondola rides on our little lake here at Council Crest were about as pretty as any you'll find. Ladies liked them too. Especially in the evening." Amos was a man maybe thirty-five, with a worldly kind of sadness about him.

"So, on your way to Seattle. You come up on the S. P.? Hoboing? There's no more Southern Pacific across the Columbia, you know. Northern Pacific takes you on to Seattle."

Amos told the big-bellied barkeep we didn't need drinks, then was properly appreciative we had biked our way up from California. He asked about the roads and what kind of weather we ran into. Ray and I took turns telling about our trip. Two men who had been talking nearby now stood behind us and listened. Ray livened to his stories, eagerly waiting for me to finish mine, even finishing for me if I hunted for the words. A third fellow, and another, stood around us and asked questions too. Before I was through telling about the Greek road gang, Ray was starting his story of the rattlesnake. With our map laid out on the bar he showed the gathering exactly where it happened.

Finally, I said we should go back to our table. "A fellow up there kindly offered to get us a drink. Said he'd wait for us."

"Short fellow? Near the main entrance?" Amos asked. "Told you he'd tell Charlie to give you an Oregon beer 'cause you're from out of town?" The men nodded and laughed, enjoying whatever was the big joke.

"That's Mort, all right. Erickson's greeter, unofficial, that is," said one fellow. The men watched us knowingly, saying, "Good old Mort," "Never takes a day off, that one," "Always looking for young hot bloods."

"Did you give him any money?" Amos asked gravely. "Make him any promises?"

"Couple of nickels," I said. "No promises," Ray added.

"Kiss those nickels goodbye," bellowed a big fellow in overalls.

"Vic, Ray." Amos was earnest. "These folks and I have been in Portland awhile. I'm in business down the street and glad for the new mayor because of the trade. But Harvey here." Amos took hold of the arm of a middle-aged man standing near. "Harvey wrote a good many pieces in the *Oregon Journal* to keep Lane in office. But good old Portland voted for Joe Simon. Soon as Simon took office the unsavories came to power with him. Mort now, he works for the "Mansion of Sin," old Madame Fanshaw's place. You know what I'm talking about, boys?"

"We do." It was Ray got his tongue to going while I still chewed on mine.

"Well, Mort is out looking for business for his ladies. But if he thinks he won't be able to interest a man in his pretty women, then he's likely to steal. And Mort's just one. There are others, plenty of them right in this saloon. My advice, you boys don't even go back to that front table for your beer, or your nickels, and consider yourselves fortunate. You might just leave right here through the side door." The others nodded, saying, "Good advice, lads," "Best be on your way," "Catch that old ferry across the river."

"Thanks," Ray said. "But Vic here left his sack on the table up front. We're grateful for the warning though." He turned to lead the way back through the thicket of drinking men whose talk was louder now, gustier than when we came in. "See that fair good and proper, lads" one of the men hollered after us. "Good luck," another yelled. We waved to them over the hats of the crowd.

Scrambling our way through the revelers was slow work. My head was in a spin: nickels, rucksack. I couldn't even remember what we'd put in Ray's sack and what we stuffed in mine. Nearer the front entrance, the new arrivals, eager to get back to the bar, were even harder to buck.

Ahead, Ray inched around a clump of roisterers, and I was finally clear of a bunch of fellows putting on their greatcoats. I made my way to Ray now standing at our table. No Mort. No white-bearded man. On the table were two empty glasses and a full ashtray. No rucksack.

Ray held out his hand. In his palm sat our witless billiken. "Left us the imp," he groaned.

27

❧ ❧ ❧

At last we reached the river, but the ferry was not due for
half an hour, so we ran foot races up and down the bridge to
keep warm until the ferry came. We could look across and see
the lights of Vancouver, and farther back the sky was
illuminated by a forest fire.

FROM THEIR LETTER TO THE *SANTA ROSA PRESS DEMOCRAT*

By the time we got back to the bikes twilight had turned to
black night. Black to match my soul. Now, pedaling down the
lamp-lighted street, the only lightness in me was on my back,
about to fly off with no rucksack to hold it down. Worse, no three
dollars and seventy-five cents, thanks to my persuading Ray I should
carry the better half of the wealth.

I now had no trusty goggles, no bandanna Mama bought me, or
my sister Olive's tin cup, the one she gave me saying it was the only
part of her would ever see that fair. The apple and jerky didn't
count, but the pack itself was like a piece of my own hide. To go off
and leave it was some cockamamie stunt; my head chock-a-block full
of craziness to see that big bar; senses on fire at finding myself in a
whale of a saloon full of grown men. Men like me, I thought.
Except I'd wager there wasn't a one under that roof would have
pulled my blear-witted trick.

To make matters more uncomfortable, all Ray said was that he
guessed losing the pack was God's good way of punishing us for
setting foot in a den of sin. Never a blame at me. But then he said,
and mostly to make me feel better, I knew, "I liked seeing that bar,
Vic, even at God's price." Nearly five miles after crossing the
Willamette River, we pedaled onto a planked trestle over the
Columbia River marshlands. At its crest, stopped astraddle our
wheels, we braced against the biting wind to gaze over the black
expanse of the river. Beyond it lights all in a line had to be the town
of Vancouver in that fabled state of Washington; the corona of
orange-red in the northeast sky must be a forest fire, a big one. But

no lights of a ferryboat moved on the water.

"Think it's already tied up for the night?" Ray was the one asked what we both feared.

"Sure would scuttle us from sleeping in a new state this night."

Road planks were even, making for a smooth coast down the trestle bridge. At the bottom lay the river's bank and the ferry landing. A small wagon and animal waited on the raised loading platform, and the driver ambled over to us. "Ferry'll be along. Half hour more or less," he said. "I keep a blanket in the wagon there. If you're cold, you boys welcome to bundle up in it till she comes."

We told him no thanks on his kind offer, and I said, "My friend and I like to run foot races, keep the blood to pumping."

And Ray and I were off. Like wild men we tore up the pitch to the bridge, the cut of the breeze a dandy goad. "On your mark," I said when we reached the planks. And we were away, up to the high point of the trestle and back down, puffing and panting. "On your mark," I yelled again, needing another try. Santa Rosa never saw the day Ray could beat me, and I couldn't believe it had just happened.

After what seemed over a half hour, but with me beating Ray more than once, a ferry's faint yellow lights grew stronger.

Winded from our run, we let the wagon driver do the talking. He lived in Washington and rode this ferry every day, and every day the ferry was late. A ditch near the Vancouver Army barracks would be a safe place for us to roll up, and some of the best fishing in the state of Washington was on the Lewis River.

Long minutes later the boat came into low, black profile against the starry night. As it neared shore the engine subsided to a hefty chug. The horn blasted twice, just before the boat bumped one side of the slip, then the other, nosing itself in. Wood groaned against wood. On board men hollered. A deck hand grabbed a hawser from around a piling and tied it to the boat one side, then same on the other. A second deck hand loosed the apron to shudder itself down, then bang on the boards of the deck. Waving behind him, the deck hand clumped toward us. Several fellows loped down the ramp and walked on past us. A horse pulling a buggy minced from the middle of the boat up to the ramp and balked. The driver swore, jumped down and led him off, the buggy clattering after.

Once the boat was unloaded, the hand motioned us forward. Taking our two ten-cent pieces, he said, "Same as two men and their animals."

We asked him if we might sit in the furnace room because of the cold. "Below." He pointed. "Through the bulkhead door. Down the passage. I'll likely see you there after we're underway. Wheels against the rail now."

Settled on overturned buckets, yelling above the roar of the behemoth of an asbestos-covered furnace and the pounding pistons, we shed our coats, then our sweaters. Soon the fare-taker and another fellow bulked in and stood about, amusing themselves and us with their stories.

After what seemed no time at all, the men put on their coats, watch caps and gloves, and the ferry thumped one side and the other, grinding and squeaking against pilings. Ray and I looked at each other. "The state of Washington," I said next to his ear.

"Washington, Vic."

Following the wagon driver's counsel, camp was in a ditch beside the high fence of the U.S. Military Reservation in Vancouver. Not far from the other side of the fence several brick buildings rose to three, four stories high.

Low overcast in the northeast sky reflected throbbing pinks and reds. The fire was a goliath. Sleep came the instant I rolled up, right after I heard Ray say my name as he prayed softly.

Next morning, at a crossroads just out of town, we took the fork straight north to La Center. Rideable, the road wound around the base of the hills through land just being cleared. To either side men burned brush in great flaming piles or grubbed out stumps. One fellow yelled at us to move along, said he was about to blow up a stump and didn't want us scared or hurt. Two great porcupines lumped out from the brush, muttering to themselves as they chased across the road faster than animals that shape ought. "This country is frontier for sure," I said. "Folks just now readying to settle."

"I have an uncle up here in Chehalis," Ray said. "He writes Mama about how Washington's new to the Union. Only been in since '89."

"We go through Chehalis?" I said, so he'd think I, along with everybody else, knew when Washington became a state.

"Road takes us right there. Promised Mama I'd look up Uncle Lloyd. Maybe they'll have us for a meal."

"Home cooking sounds fine."

The surface still graded, we pedaled side by side and watched the east mountains come in and out of view as the smoke collected and thinned.

Ray said, "Saddle sores are about to make a foot soldier of me, Vic."

"Saddle sores? Didn't know you had saddle sores."

"Just before Portland they got bad. Thought they'd get better. Guess not."

"What do you do for saddle sores?"

"Stand up," he said, and stood to pedal. But after a bridge, the road became a bed of rocks under thick dust and we got off to walk anyway.

"Pa used to tell about his pa," I said. "How when he was in the Cavalry in the Civil War, they used to pump pus out of saddle sores with a jar rim. Suction sucked it right out."

"Couldn't hurt worse than I hurt now. Got a jar?" Poor guy was having a time of it. I saw now he shifted about even while he walked, different from the hobble he sometimes used to protect his trick ankle.

North of La Center the road got seriously awful. Short, steep grades, up and down both. Then the surface turned to deep sand.

I said, "We best look for camp. Work on those sores in daylight."

"Plenty of light left. The road should get closer to the river on ahead. Be good to wake up and see it first thing." The sand petered out and we mounted, but after a turn or two the road narrowed to barely wider than the two deep ruts that sprouted boulders big as dog carts. On shank's mare again and pushing around a jagged rock, I said, "Just remembered that bottle of Orino's Laxative Mama shoved on me. I'll empty it. Rim should be about right."

"You're a regular pal, Vic."

Up the steepest pitch yet, we stopped to eat berries from the giant vines growing over the inside ditch. But now the clouds that had been fattening lowered and turned the color of lead. Light and scattered at first, the rain all at once thumped like pebbles, and we rummaged for our coats. Road dirt turned to thick, gummy mud.

The walk down the other side was between ruts more like young rivers, with us now as muddy as our rigs. After crossing a bridge at the bottom of the grade we had ourselves a fine laugh just looking at each other. And a harder one when I told Ray he must have put God up to all this so's he wouldn't have to sit on his festering nether cheeks.

At the next summit we stopped to look down on a fine broad flow of water that glinted gold in a patch of sun. "Woodland ferry crossing the Lewis River," Ray said, digging in his pack for coins.

"That wagon driver said fishing's good here. Want to make camp?"

"Too much day left, Vic."

At the river's edge we stood on the log corduroy landing-apron to watch the relic of a raft-like craft jerk its way across the swiftly moving water. "Poor old girl must have been here to meet Lewis and Clark," I said. Ray needed a laugh.

Scarcely bigger than a wagon, the ferry groaned nearer. One corner dipped crazily under water when the current took it on a sideways hitch. A couple of broad-shouldered fellows hauled at the cable that ran in pulleys along the side until finally they crunched the rickety thing hard up to the apron.

"Fifteen cents each." One of the fellows pocketed Ray's three dimes. The other fellow walked up the hill, apparently a passenger. We pushed the bikes onto the raft and laid them down in the middle.

"You're strong lads," the fare taker said. "Be obliged if you'd help cable us over." The current romped along, stronger than appeared from the bank. In the middle of the river, the three of us putting our full weight into the pull, the boat still crabbed sideways.

On the other side a wagon waited to load, and we pushed off up the sandy grade from the river. The ferryman yelled, "Thanks for the hands," and we waved back.

In the town of Woodland where we stopped at a pump, I said, "Come near twenty-five miles today. Not one of 'em easy. And there's not much day left." Ray filled his canteen, then his cup. "Should have enough light to get where we can see that old Columbia in the morning, Vic." And not two months ago I worried Ray wouldn't be able to keep up.

Out of town we took a left fork at a board with an arrow saying "Kelso." The surface was passable, and we mounted, with me in the lead. It was at the bottom of the first hill that I heard, behind me, a sharp crack. The sickening snap of metal. I spun around. Ray's bicycle was lopped over like some wounded thing. He stood by it, tube and handlebars swinging free in his sad grip.

28

⊕ ⊕ ⊕

For about two miles there was a steep grade with rocks here
and there which a horse would find hard to climb over.

FROM THEIR LETTER TO THE *SANTA ROSA PRESS DEMOCRAT*

We just sat there in the dirt. "Snapped off clean," Ray said,
gazing at the broken corpse.

"Roads are too foul for any natural-built bicycle," I said and
glanced sideways at him. Tears brimmed his eyes. "We barely have
money to get up there, Vic. None for a brazier."

"We'll strap the thing together and carry it. Trade bikes every
little bit." Suddenly I felt bone-weary and sick with uncertainty.
Myself with no rucksack. Ray's wheel now a wounded soldier. His
backside full of pus. Closer than ever to that fair, and I never felt
farther away. I dug in a saddlebag for belts and rope, while I stole
another look. A tear coursed down his cheek. Ray, along with his
bike, could be about to fold on me.

"You got your mama's five dollars," I said. "Plus our three
dollars and twenty cents. That's money enough for a brazier and
then some. Hey, the Columbia's back." I pointed west to the band
of water that showed through nearby oaks and cottonwoods.
"Another mile or so we'll make camp close to the bank. See big
water when we wake up."

Ray carrying the strapped-up cripple and still mighty quiet, we set
out. I rode down the next short incline, and at the double-back got
off to walk. Down the hill toward us a team of two pulled a wide
grading rig that raised a mountain of dust, though the road was still
crusted from the rain. The fellow driving hollered he'd come from
Kalama and was about to turn around and make the run back.
"Camp here you can start out in the morning on a smooth road
that's had the night to settle." He began to bring the animals about
for a wide swing at the hairpin.

Alongside, Ray seemed embarrassed, though I could guess the
grader fellow scarcely noticed his patched-up bike. I yelled thanks as

he completed his turn. "We'll try the tracks awhile. Use your settled road in the morning." Ray looked dubious, eyeing down to the left where the railroad serpentined.

I said, "As easy to carry bikes down there as up here." He peered to the west. The river was blanked by clumps of maples and willows. "Columbia's out there. Map shows the tracks run close to it. And there's still light." His voice was alive. "Besides, tracks'll be blessed level," I said. "How far you think to Kalama?" "Near six miles. But we can camp by the river sooner than that." He sounded almost himself.

It was a scramble down the bank. The bikes hung up on everything, salal, young alder, bracken, berry vines. We fought ourselves and the wheels through the tangle, over and around the boulders, and without Ray's bicycle coming apart. Finally we stumbled off the bank, then slogged through several hundred feet of swampy sludge before we could heft ourselves onto the rail bed, built up so the tracks lay on a sort of low trestle. To either side marsh growth looked to be cattails and heavy grass. "If a train comes through, no place to jump," Ray worried.

We tried to match our stride to the ties but mostly failed, our gait lurching even more when we shifted the bikes from one side to the other. Before long the mud below turned to mucky water, cattail sticks and razor-edged grass swaying and rustling in the slow breeze from the river.

The green of the western sky had turned shades of pink and lavender where it showed through a tumble of slate-colored clouds. Light would go fast. But off to the right I could see the road pitch and yaw up and down those short steep grades and reminded myself to be glad for the level.

After a long straight piece, we changed wheels. The carrying weight was the same, but his was harder to manage, the grabbing of it different so's it wouldn't wrench apart. With my wheel he moved to the lead. I hollered up, "Could be you carried on too much in those prayers of yours, asking deliverance from saddle riding so's you could—and I sing-songed—coddle those cankers on your crupper." He looked over his shoulder, a good smile still left in him.

An occasional piece of land was dry enough for willows and low growth, but around them water stood in swampy bogs. A wet dunk waited for us if we had to bail off for a train. Then would be the time to worry if the water was over our heads, and we'd see if loaded bicycles would float.

"Rail station," Ray pointed ahead. The sign on the end of the small building read "Martin's Bluff." He was ginger about laying his bicycle down on the board platform, but more ginger about sitting himself on the bench, easing onto one cheek then the other. Scanning the posted schedule, I announced, "No trains 'til tomorrow." He stood up in stages, adjusting his trousers on the way. Best I get that putrid pus out of him tonight.

We'd no more started down the tracks than that giant Columbia showed itself, a broad, shining belt interrupted by what appeared islands, a small one close to the near bank, a bigger one farther out, both lush with growth.

The tracks now were about twenty feet from the river's bank. In the near water a couple of mergansers dove for their dinner. They bobbed back up like roly toys, each with a twisting fish in its hooked bill, then downed them in a gulp. We scanned for dry land, spying at the same moment a shelf a short way down the bank that nosed out into the water. Camp.

The glow of a gone day was mostly a purple and blue memory in the western sky. "Too dark to fish," Ray said and pulled jerky from his pack.

Mostly by leftover light off the water I operated on his poor backside. Six dollar-sized sores gave up their load to the Orino Laxative jar, with him yelping like a hooty man each time I pressed the rim into his sad old bottom. After I'd cleaned them with carbolic acid, I sat back on my haunches. "These rascals got you put off the road awhile, chum. Gonna have to use your mama's five dollars. Get you to Chehalis on the train to your uncle's. Give your behind time to fix." He just lay there on his stomach watching the ducks. "Eat some of your aunt's cooking. Put your bicycle to rights. No sense makin' these doozies any madder by getting 'em infected." Ray propped on an elbow. "Best you take the three dollars and twenty cents too. Can't think what I'd buy between here and Chehalis. I can make it up there by day after tomorrow. Meet you at the Post Office."

"Me ride the train?" He sat up sideways, eyes smokey with hurt. "No, we do this trip together. Besides, it's bad business you traveling alone." I took his bedroll off his bike frame and tossed it to him. "Got no choice, Ray. Those blossoms on your bum are just asking to fester so's you won't be able to walk the rest of the way to Seattle, let alone ride. Your mama'd want you to use the money to get yourself and that wheel mended." He unrolled his blanket, not looking at me. "I can make it. I'll travel faster alone anyhow, with you in the shape you're in. To keep our word with old Finley I best see one wheel goes the distance. Road might even be good enough I can ride some." I tried to sound like I'd thought it through.

Lying there on his side, he grunted.

From where we rolled up under the brow of the bank we could watch the boats, their lights on now, as they plowed up and down the river. Tugs pulled great log rafts and chuffed like railroad engines; freighters with deep throbbing motors were stacked with milled lumber; among the several small fishing boats men yelled jolly conversations back and forth. An excitement eager as the current ran up and down this Columbia.

The river and our worries put sleep in a poor third for both of us. Ray was mostly quiet until he said, "Fur traders canoed up this old waterway a hundred years ago, Vic. On their way to Astoria. Loaded with pelts."

"Pelts and liquor. And Indian maidens."

He laughed a good laugh. I'd miss this buddy of mine. But, Ray's God helping, I'd make the near sixty miles to Chehalis by day after tomorrow. We snugged our blankets closer against the bitter breeze that now gusted through the river's channel. "Should have looked for better shelter," I said.

"Sores don't hurt as much now, Vic."

"Good."

"I'll be at the Chehalis Post Office day after tomorrow. You should get there by afternoon, sooner if you can ride. We could stay with my uncle a couple of days. Give us time to make sure the bike's going to stay soldered. Eat some home cooking. Still have almost a week to make Seattle, time for a fine look before that fair closes middle of October. From Chehalis it's only some better than a hundred miles."

"Sounds fine," I said, feeling as unsure, as unfine, as ever I could remember. A shiver took me, and I tried not to think of tomorrow, of traveling by myself through this raw land.

At the first glimmer of light over the east hills we were up and packing. "You could need all eight dollars and twenty cents," I told him. "Train fare, brazier."

"Uhhm," he grunted.

"Better than thirty miles yesterday," I said. "Eight hundred forty-nine miles now from old Santa Rosa."

"Feels like more," he mumbled.

As we hefted our packed bicycles and our weary selves onto the tracks, the eastern sky was pale green changing to yellow. "From here we go two ways, Vic."

"But you're catching the train in Kalama."

"No. Closer back to Martin's Bluff."

Our eyes held for a moment. "I'll keep the money, but I won't need it all," he said. Digging down a saddlebag, he pulled up the rest of the jerky and handed it to me. Down again and out came the billiken. "My stand-in." I stuffed the lump in my trouser pocket. I didn't turn to watch Ray, just listened to his footfalls heading south. I knew he didn't turn either, but I walked the gravel between the ties so's he'd track me by the sound too.

After a time that was long enough for him to make it to Martin's Bluff, I pulled off for a northbound train to pound by and looked hard for Ray at a window. But he was likely on an inside seat. Later I learned that just as he arrived at the station the train was pulling out. Poor guy had to wait until four o'clock that afternoon for another.

My solitary footfalls sounded too loud on the gravel, on the ties. Heading north. Alone. Through unknown country. I thought I remembered animals would stalk one person where they mightn't stalk two. But bears, cougars were likely to stalk from the woods. No bother in this marshland. Would Ray truly be fit to make the trip on to Seattle from Chehalis? Would I, could I, go the distance by myself? At a stretch of solid ground, I left the tracks and aimed for the road. Heavy scrub under the trees made for slow going, but after maybe a quarter mile, I found the road.

In Kalama I stopped to fill the canteen and eat some plums, then ambled around to the back of a bakery and asked for some day-old biscuits. The fellow brought out a full flour sack and said I could take four.

A long trestle, then a bridge, led to and crossed the wide Kalama River, a mighty lot of water that moved along at a fine rate. The sun toasting my back and the bike greasing along the level bridge, I could almost believe Chehalis would be a quick jaunt. Soon the road swung under a railroad trestle, and I was on foot. Up a steep, rocky grade, down another with more rocks, these as big as packing crates. Just when I thought the boulders were the worst of it, I met a grade at least 25 per cent, a road standing on its head. When I'd pushed up that one, most of the breath was gone from me. But at the top I walked out onto a bluff, and the view sucked out the rest.

That granddaddy of a river down there coursed from south to northwest on its heavy journey to the sea, along its way encircling islands themselves as broad as most rivers. I watched it work, that old waterway doing what it was meant to. I looked hard so I might tell Ray every detail. Then, before I asked them, my lips started forming words I figured he would say to his God.

29

❋　❋　❋

The country was very wild looking and very few people lived
there. . . . The day was now about half over and I was
beginning to get lonesome. For the next ten miles a little path
by the side of the railroad was found much better than the
wagon road.

FROM A LETTER TO THE *SANTA ROSA PRESS DEMOCRAT*

For the next three miles downgrade was as bad as up, just as
steep and full of boulders, a hefty push or a tussle to hold the
wheel back. I met one horse and rider, but he was a youngster
in a rush to get on to Kalama and didn't want to talk. At the
bottom of one grade, log corduroy stretched across a marsh, and for
those several hundred feet it was mighty sweet just to bump over
logs. With no up or down I could think my worries about if I had to
walk all the way to Chehalis, and how would I meet Ray at the Post
Office by any time tomorrow?

Woods as dense as any I'd seen lined the road on either side.
Dark enough, thick enough for a bear to hide in. Ahead, a covey of
jaunty quail paraded peep-peeping across the road to disappear in
the brush. "Hey you, wait up," I hollered at them, then felt some
foolish and looked behind me, half hoping for a walker, even to
catch me talking to a bunch of birds.

But back there, just more nothing: road, woods, a swearing jay.
What a chumpy idea this was, trying to wheel a thousand miles to
see a fair. Now Ray was too saddle-sore to ride and his bike was in
pieces. Worst of all, he'd been vanquished into taking the train. And
I'd forced him to do it. This was a sad day. We had broken our
promise to the paper and Santa Rosa, not to mention ourselves.

Feeling wretched, I stopped at an outside turn to study the dust
and a cluster of horseshoe-shaped elk prints all sizes. No scoop to
their tracks, the animals not on the move.

Ahead, a trestle bridged a deep ravine, and I stopped astride the
bike, drawing in breath. I had no time for frets. A road trestle with

its side railing and broad board tracks was mother's comfort compared to a railroad trestle with skinny rails perched atop frail-looking latticework. Besides, a high-up trestle was as safe as a low one. No more danger for a single bike than for two. My stomach thought different.

I headed out, aiming for the raised boards of the left track. Look only in front of the wheel, not at the cross boards and their deep down spaces between. With a mighty grip on the bars, my wheel and I had thumped nearly across when a great slam-boom thundered from high up on the facing hill. I stopped dead and raised my eyes to see the biggest bucked log in all creation come lickety-splitting down a steep chute of peeled logs that ran alongside the road ahead. The whopping tree trunk shot by, rumbling and screeching, to pound hard somewhere below, likely a skid road leading to a mill. The log must have been sixty feet long, and at least eight feet in diameter. Ray would hear about this one.

Once off the trestle bridge a dandy graded road greased me along. Only one hand on the bars and hankering for a voice, I sang "The Star Spangled Banner" all the way through. Then all the way through again, while the four or so miles to Kelso flew behind me.

Without Ray's pocket watch I couldn't know just when I arrived in town, but the day looked early to middle afternoon. At a trough and pump I washed and filled the canteen. A burly fellow with a Swedish accent stopped to ask where I was headed. When I told him north he said, "Road's terrible rough. You'd do better on the trail next to the tracks this side of the river. Road and tracks follow the Cowlitz one side and the other." I told him I was much obliged, that I would take his advice. He was right, I rode for long stretches on the level path beside the tracks, getting off only when brush grew out too far or a rock bulked. Still, I felt more alone here than I would across the river on that miserable road where I'd at least have the chance to meet a traveler, pass some words.

About five miles out of Kelso, the sun teetering on the west hills, there was plenty of light left to make Castle Rock and maybe farther before darkness forced me to camp. Bumping along the trail, I sang, then took a deep breath for a good yodel. Before letting it out, I listened. From under me came a soft, sad hiss-ss-ss. Then, like a fat man punched in the belly, with a great gasp my front tire died itself flat. The day about to expire on me, now my tire did the same.

I scrambled off, frustration building to near sickness, and settled myself, tools, kit and wheel next to the trail. A whopper of a piece of glass had cut clean through both tire and tube. In record time—for me—I was patched and back on the bike, the sun now but a fiery glow above the hill. Another twenty minutes of light used up. All song gone from me, I listened to the evening warble of a bird telling the world he was about to lay it down.

Somehow I crossed three nerve-killing trestles before I pushed in to Castle Rock with dusk about to claim the day. At the bakery I walked around back, but it was closed. Munching a plum, I put my coat on. With no sun the air took on a healthy nip. At a trough I waited for a wagon driver to fill his canteen and offered him a plum. He took it, thanked me, then complained about having to make Kelso by nightfall. "At least the road south is better than the road north," he told me. "Keep to the tracks, boy, is this man's advice," and he swung up onto his seat. I watched him pull out, just as a train whistled its approach to town.

The cyclometer read eight hundred seventy-two. Twenty-four miles today. If Ray's calculation was right, I had at least another thirty-five to Chehalis. Too many for tomorrow on the railroad path. Too many by road, if I believed the wagon driver, and I did. Even in twilight I could make a few miles by the tracks, cut some for tomorrow. With a train now going through, another wouldn't likely come along soon. Besides, anything was better than making camp.

Just out of town the road bridged from the west side of the river to the east, same side as the rails. If I decided, I should have no trouble finding the road. Again on the path next to the tracks, I pointed my wheel north. Dusk was settling, but the gas lamp should throw light enough, if it came to that. I rode fast as the path allowed, ducking overhangs, dodging the biggest rocks. But now shadows took form too late, making a liar of me when I dodged a boulder that wasn't there, or ran smack into a low branch that was. I dismounted. A sane man would roll up, start out in the morning. But I'd sooner camp near the road, closer to whatever travel might happen along.

Darkness was coming on, and I eyed the hillside above me, heavy with growth. No telling now if the road was still up there. Better I should stay where I was until I could be sure just where the road lay. No sense wandering about in wild country at night wrestling a loaded bike. I'd wait for a likely clearing on the hillside and strike off for the road. Then my heart flew to my mouth. Ahead, in the near dark, the unmistakable outlines of a trestle. I looked up at the steep, shadowy hill. Should I tackle it, try to find the road? With my headlamp, I should have less trouble on the trestle. Once on the other side, I'd look for the road.

Very near the crossing I put my ear to the rail. Cold, hard, no hum. As though my insides had eyes, they knew this trestle was a high one and likely long. I struck a match and fired up the headlamp, its jewel windows sending a fine glow in front and to the sides. Once underway on the hollow-sounding boards, I realized my mistake: the light cast brilliance where I didn't need it and shadows where I did. I reached forward to turn off the lamp, but felt suddenly unbalanced. I withdrew my hand, so carefully. Besides, I could be worse off without the light. To turn around was out of the question. To back up was impossible. Forward was my only choice.

The bounce of the boards wrenched the light this way and that, brightening then shading objects I didn't recognize. Distance became close, while the next step disappeared. Halfway, maybe, across, I stopped. Standing fixed, confusion rippled through me. I couldn't cross. I could not take another step. I wanted to crawl, but what of the bike? I could sit down, but where to lay the wheel? I'd crossed trestles before. Forget the light. Don't look. Just know the next step. Remember the sound. Slowly, I breathed in, out. Feeling returned to my legs, feet. Inch by careful inch, I pushed the bike, and stepped, ahead, pushed, stepped. Don't watch the lamplight, sense the next step. Inch, by inch. How long would Ray wait before he sent help to look for me? At once, reflecting light, the ground was no more than six feet below. Feeling returned to my hands. Slowly, they released their steel-grip on the bars.

Safely across, quivering all over, I flopped the wheel down and slumped beside it, head in my hands.

"Halloo there! Halloo?"

I jerked up, looked about. Above and off to the right, a lantern swung side to side.

"I say, you in trouble? You with the downed lamp?"

30

❄ ❄ ❄

Finally a buggy came by that was going to Toledo, so I
followed it to keep on the road. The driver whipped the horse
all the way, up hill and down, and it was all I could do to stay
on the wheel and keep pace with him. I hit rocks, ruts and
everything but the soft spots.

FROM A LETTER TO THE *SANTA ROSA PRESS DEMOCRAT*

Aye-e-e, you took quite a toomble. That slope is a steep one,
r-r-right enough." The Scottish accent was as welcome as the
light from his lantern that swung in rhythm to his long
strides down the hill. "Those outside curves, they ar-re most
treacherous, the worse if you've not met them befor-re. Ooay-ee,
can you walk?" Reaching me, his large hand supported my elbow.

"I didn't tumble off the road, sir. Just stopped to rest after
crossing the trestle." On my feet, embarrassed, I righted the wheel,
then doused my lamp in favor of his lantern.

"You have braw pluck, laddie. I'd not be crossing one of them
trestles till the world be blessed with daylight, and then only after a
mighty flogging. Follow me along. We'll be for a trek to the road."
With that he barged up the hillside in lunges lusty as the ones
coming down.

A titan this fellow was, well over six feet, with bushy red hair and
beard that looked quite fierce in the sharp lantern light. But
likeable, his burr so thick I had to listen hard to mine the words. I
followed after him up the bank, through the thick undergrowth and
small trees, hefting the bicycle high as I could, but not high
enough; a saddlebag hung up first thing. I stopped to pull it loose
and hollered, "Dark came on quicker than I planned, or I'd have
been on the road in the first place," feeling a need to explain. In my
struggle to keep up with his light, I lowered the bike, only to have a
wheel snag a young fir. No amount of tugging freed it. From higher
up, his lantern shone full on me. "Thanks," I yelled, untangling the
bike.

"You are a detair-r-mined lad," the man called, directing the beam to help me negotiate the last few yards. Finally I dragged myself and bike up onto the road and dropped my burden on its wheels.

"I'm R-Robert. Bound nor-rth aboot a mile. You?"

"North, too. Name's Victor." We set off then, my huge friend walking the narrow outside shoulder, while I took the inside. I told him where I was going and where I'd come from and enjoyed his roar of startlement.

With each gigantic stride his lantern blared first at the wall of forest ahead, then plunged us into dark thick as a black cat's insides. Grades were steep and the road rutted, but the company of this big fellow put a lift in my spirits.

"To car-ry a lantern is not my habit, most every turn and pebble like my own bairn. I car-ry it now, for last night, r-right about here-re, a banshee of a cougar screamed from the bank just above my ear-r. Followed along beside me it did, eyes like fireballs."

"Cougar? They known to attack a man?"

"Big cats do most feast on deer and sheep. But farmers thr-rough here have come to shelter their animals in the cote of a night. So, poor cougar must find himself another-r meal." Again he guffawed, while I shivered. "Don't be fr-retting, lad. With the light of the lantern and the two of us together Sir Cougar will look for a safer meal this night, aye."

Suddenly he stopped. To the right I made out a cut through the heavy woods. "I'll be off now on my wee drive. Would you be kind enough to do me the honor of sleeping on my cabin's floor? It's well past good light and the r-road gets no better."

"Thanks, but I'd like to make Toledo before bedding down. I have to meet my friend in Chehalis tomorrow."

He glanced up at the scant half-moon. "It's nigh eleven o'clock, lad. Late for safe travel. Chehalis will come in its time."

"I do thank you for your offer, sir. But I'll rest easier with a few more miles behind me." And we shook hands.

Around the first bend I fumbled down a bag for a match and the tin of carbide. Then stuffed them back as I heard the clatter of a rig and snort of an animal coming up fast. Rounding the turn in a prodigious hurry, the driver then roared right past me, slapping reins to the horse even as he went. I pushed out right after him, following close as I could to use the dancing light from his rig's lanterns fixed to either side. If I could keep up, I might trick a cougar into thinking I was part of the assembly.

But the driver was a wild man. He whipped his horse all the way up the grade. I pushed fast, dodging some ruts, bumping down more. Still, the light was a help, and I didn't hanker to fall back, maybe turn into cougar bait. The buggy pell-melled, rattling and bouncing down the next grade, the driver flailing his hapless horse to a near gallop, the animal heaving and blowing. Up the next grade and down, the fellow stung that critter's hide, while I fought to stay mounted, slamming into rocks, puffing hard as the horse. Of a sudden the surface was unrolled gravel. Off they charged, lighting their way through the darkness. The gravel slowed me to a stop.

Again I dug in the bag for the carbide tin and a match. The five hours of burn from the last loading had to be near gone. Faint moonlight proved enough to pour the granules into the chamber and, from my canteen, the bit of needed water. The two-minute wait for the gas to form proved more than enough time to regret, most deeply, refusing Scotty's cabin floor.

I struck the match on my trousers and put it to the aperture. White flame shot high and bright. I was glad for the convex lens that shone strong light wide into the next turn. My fingers traced a side bag, following the line of the revolver. I unbuckled the buckle and pushed off through gravel that fought back.

Two wheel revolutions and I stopped, listened. Most surely I'd heard a cougar scream, but at a distance. Again. Closer? Pushing hard, I was tired as ever I could remember and lonely as a man should ever find himself. Any moment now I could take the place of some miserable sheep in a big cat's belly. I plowed on through the damnable gravel, pushed up a grade, lurched down the other side. Couldn't mount. Impossible to run. My fingers circled the cool barrel of the .32. Around a hairpin the winding road tunneled through trees so high they sheltered it from the pale moon. All was blackness save for my lamp, converting the road and side forests into jerky, jagged chunks of light and shadow. In the flat dark, cold night air cut deep. I hunched against it, glad my coat. Gravel dragged at every step and wheel turn; the bike grew weightier; my bones were sick with fatigue.

Again I stopped to listen. Another animal. This time, a yip like a fox. Then ahead, off to the side, twin live-ember eyes glinted in my beam, two burning holes piercing the pitchy night. They disappeared. I turned the handlebars, directing the beam where the eyes had been. You shouldn't run from a wild animal, I thought I remembered. Or was it more dangerous to stand still? Ray would know. I was off and pushing, my eyes burning their own holes in the jet wall beside the road, searching for a motion or a sense of motion, or a pair of live-coal eyes or, heaven help, a thing I mightn't conjure. My ears strained, to the back, front, sides.

Of a sudden, the gravel quit; back to blessed ruts and rocks. Mounting, I bounced down the grade, then dismounted for the up. Surely Toledo wasn't much farther. Tired as I was, frightened as I was, still my body wouldn't hold out much longer without rest. This could be a time to say one of those prayers to Ray's God. Abruptly, on the same side as before, two red-yellow eyes caught in my light. Closer than before, larger, on the bank almost above me. I froze. I couldn't move, couldn't think. In a twitch the eyes were gone. Mine stayed riveted to the black where they'd been, my muscles rigid, breath closed off. The air, the woods, all still as stone. Not a movement, not a sound in this inkwell of a night.

Gradually, muscle by muscle, they were mine again. I walked the bike fast and as quietly as ever I could, listening all ways. I slid the revolver's trigger lock. How long would a hungry cougar follow a prey before it pounced? Stealthily, I pushed up the grade. Death by animal attack. Was it like getting yanked by the collar, just before the nothingness? Or, after the red, searing pain, was death gentle, like a smother under heavy blankets? If I did have time to react, could I control the gun? Pushing, cringing at each thump down a rut, I was suddenly cold, very cold, and my eyes ached for probing the blackness.

Without being truly aware, I had reached the crest. There below, a light, no, two lights, bobbed, and yes, reflected in water. I didn't remember Ray saying the road crossed the Cowlitz ahead of Toledo. But the lights looked to be lanterns hung from the end of a sure-enough barge ferry on the other side of the river. Praise be to the Lord and maybe billiken. Brought abruptly to life, I mounted for the down. The daddy of all chuck holes threw me first thing, and off I hopped, my heart still thudding relief. Half-walking, half-running, I stumbled the bike down the steep grade to the river.

At the planking of the ferry approach I looked across at the lights lifting and dropping with the pulse of the water. The barge itself though, looked more anchored into than tied up at the bank, the way its stern end only lifted and sank and didn't swing at all.

"Last crossing was, uh, uh, midnight," a sleepy drawl called huskily from the other side of the river. "No more till morning."

"I must cross tonight, sir. Please?" I shouted over the grumble of the water.

"Ferry's hung up. Damn-n-n buggy I just brought o-o-ver. Horse spooked, and the dern—"

"I'm alone. Could you maybe take me in a skiff, sir?" Suddenly I was desperate. I couldn't spend the night on this river bank with God knows what or who stalking me.

The river rushed louder and softer. The night grew blacker outside my lamp light and that of the wavering lanterns. The fellow must have fallen asleep. I might wake him with a shout, and I drew a lungful. Then the voice bawled a sort of non-word, followed by a slurred, "You—got—money? For—fare?" It hit me: Ray had all our money. I was sentenced to stay on this side, together with whatever waited for me. Tomorrow, if I had one, I might talk my way into a hitch across in some wagon bed, or find the railroad so I could walk a trestle. But as for tonight. . . .

What would Ray do, I wondered, if I just never showed up at the Chehalis Post Office?

31

⚜ ⚜ ⚜

The ferry had just taken a buggy over and had got stuck in
the sand, so he came back in a row boat. I finally got my
wheel in the back end of the boat and shoved out into the
stream. There was quite a current and it being pretty dark we
could not see where we were going.

FROM A LETTER TO THE *SANTA ROSA PRESS DEMOCRAT*

Driven by stark fear and a panic at having to spend what was
left of the night either pacing the river bank, or bedding
down as a prone and weakened victim, I gave one last holler,
"I have no money, sir. But I have goods of worth." My words
trailed off, lost in the water's clamor, sounding every bit the lie they
were. No answer. If the ferryman wasn't asleep, he probably chose
not to risk himself on a black night in heavy water for no fare. Who
could blame him?

My fate now clear, I trained my lamp on the rocky bank, then the
planking of the ferry approach. Boards would give a flat surface at
least. I could hope a wild thing might stay shy of man-made planks,
and that my tuckered body would sleep, in spite of my head
knowing better. I doused the lamp, laid the bike down on the
boards and unrolled the blanket.

On my hands and knees, smoothing the blanket over the rough
planks, I stiffened. Above the steady, low-order roar of swiftly
moving water, a thud, then another, louder than the first. I gripped
the revolver and unlocked the trigger. Again from the dark river, a
stout thump and grind of wood. Oars in oar locks. I breathed again.

"Gol—darn." The strung-out words were close by. "Where's the
dern—lamp?" Oars banged gunnels. "I'm here, sir," I sang out and
relocked the trigger, but saw only black night and the nervous rays
from the lanterns across the water. "Why'd you kill your lamp?" A
small boat ground gravel down river of the planks. "Get in—darn
ya." Caught in the flickering light, a short figure stood near the

middle of a skiff, grabbed for an overhanging limb, missed and plopped down. "Before—the con-sarn river—takes me out again."

"Yes, sir." I was already carrying the bike and blanket over the rocks to where the bow end of a rowboat crunched with every surge of water.

"A wheel? Tarnation! Can't take—that across! You never said nothin' 'bout a gol-derned bike! And it loaded to beat—all."

"The bags make it look bigger, sir. They'll mash down." "Jam the thing—aft here. You want to cross—you figure how to fit—them gangly shanks around all that—duffel."

A slight, wiry man, he leaned himself back and lowered the oars into the shallow water to give me more room. Then he lurched to the side and an oar came slashing out of the water. The whole operation jerked the boat free of its mooring to send it bobbing away from shore. "Fool—kid!" He spluttered. "Pull—'er 'round 'fore I'm back out to—sea."

"Yes, sir." Propping the bike against the bank, the blanket draped over it, I waded after the skiff that danced in a half circle barely out of reach. Oddly, the fellow just sat, swaying with the boat, oars dragging. His unsteady motions, thick speech; the man wasn't only sleepy, he was drunk. Here I'd pleaded and whined so a souse in a row boat could be my lifeline across a swift-running river in the wee hours of a dark night. Poor sot couldn't manage to dock his barge. What would he do to a piled-high skiff with no lanterns?

Water sloshing over my shoe-tops, I caught the stern and hauled the boat to shore, then managed to swing it about for loading. My skipper could be dozing. I threw the blanket on the seat board, then hefted the bike. Space from the man's straight-out, spindly legs to the blunt stern was skimpy. The boat was a homemade job. Though the fellow sat in the middle of his seat, the rig had a built-in list. Still, it was likely caulked to a fare-thee-well. Bottom boards felt dry as I jimmied and crammed. My front wheel perched over his knees; no amount of work or hope would fit the whole bike in the boat. The rear wheel was obliged to hang over the end, and a bag, the one without the revolver, bulged fat over a gunnel, it only about eight inches above water line. With me in, freeboard would shorten even more.

"Kee—ripes!" The fellow jolted himself straight, belched loudly, and scrabbled around at his feet. With a wild yank he brought up a third oar. "Here." He thrust it at me. "Don't use it 'less I say." Slowly we swung into the main body of the broad river.

I was still sorting myself out when the current took us. Water slapped the sides, then spun the boat endwise to carry us, stern forward, at a wild cant downstream. Slosh over the sides drenched most of what wasn't already soaked with the water I'd brought in. A hand tight around the bike frame, my other gripping the oar, I waited for my order.

"Dag nab—current. Black as a—witch's heart." An oar banged the gunnel as he fought to bring us around. But the boat raised high, a swell shooting us ahead even faster through the utter darkness. My bike shifted and strained.

"Now?" I cried.

"Stay put!" He growled.

Against the dimming barge lights, the silhouette of his spidery figure strained to one side, the other. Slowly then, groaning, the fellow brought us about, finally angling into a cross course. I ran a hand over the wheel. Frame, handlebars, of a piece so far as I could feel. The bag resting over the gunnel was soaked, of course.

"Fool bicycle. Gaggle-shanked kid. I got no brain, takin' you on." Drunk as he might have been, this tough little man now sounded near to sober, thank the Lord.

A swell slammed into us. The boat lifted, then slapped down stern forward again. "Blast!" he shouted. Once more the current swept us downstream. Feeble barge lights blinked behind foliage, then vanished, as we rounded a bend. The boat lofted and spanked down, lifted, dropped, as we sped through blackness. Then, in a manner I'll never know, the scrawny little ferryman, huffing like a spent horse, worked us out of the midstream into the slower side waters. He swiveled and peered into the dark behind him, coaxing the boat, bow forward, toward the bank.

"Fine job, mister," was all I could think to say before my head was in a tangle of brush as the boat dragged. Twigs and branches caught my cap; snagged bags snapped free and snagged again, as the fellow poled us by jerks toward the bank. Nosing into the thicket, the bottom scraped and we stopped dead.

"Climb those bones out. Find us a tie-up."

I scrambled from under the bike and over the side. With my jackknife I cut away the worst of the snare of willow branches.

"Rope's forward!" he shouted next to my ear. Ankle-deep, trying for footing in the rocky shallows, I pulled the rope out from under the bow. Overhead, a gnarled cluster of limbs led to one sturdy enough for the tie. "We're secure." Wading to the stern, I struggled to free the bike.

Finally, I lifted the drenched assembly out of the boat, draping the soaked blanket atop the rear wheel. The overhang didn't allow my holding the outfit high, and it proved heavier than my arms could manage. I lowered it, resting the bike on the gunnel to adjust my grip.

The fellow didn't offer help—not that I expected him to—just climbed out. Hefting the bike again, I pulled and dragged it through the mash of brushy growth, at last slogging myself and gear up onto the bank to set the bike down on firm ground, which was a sort of path.

"Solid walk from here," he assured, and led the way. I followed, slowly, along what must have been a trail before growth claimed it. Mostly I carried my outfit over the boulders and around and under the heavy brush.

"Goods of worth gonna pay your fare, you say?" he yelled over his shoulder. "What be they, boy?"

"I have a fine jackknife, as you just saw." I sighed at the thought of losing it. But what else could I afford to give up?

"Jackknife. I'd take a good jackknife. What else you got?"

"The knife's all I can give, mister. I need everything else for my trip." I caught up to him where he was stopped at the joining of our path with the road leading down to the ferry. His face, etched sharply in the rise and fall of the lanterns' light, showed the craggy features and deep lines of a man older than I had thought.

"I'm obliged for the crossing, mister. It was a first-rate job. The knife is quality. Sharp. Two blades." I set the bike down and dug in the side bag where I'd dropped the knife.

"I was thinking you might have a gun."

"Can't give you my gun. Belongs to my friend," I lied, pulling out the knife. With it came the billiken, falling to the ground. I picked the thing from the dirt, dropped it in the bag, and held out the knife. He took it. "What's that you dropped?"

"Just a good luck piece. Belongs to my friend too."

"Looked like one of them billikens from the Seattle Fair."

"Yes. No value to it."

"If I had one of them I could say to folks I'd been up there to the fair. You won't give me the gun, I'll settle for the billiken. That and the knife'll do. Crossing was a bad one. After hours. Disturbed my sleep." He slipped the knife in a trouser pocket, then stood watching me, a small grin starting on his face, as he held out his hand. This man was going to give me trouble if I didn't fork over the billiken. I grabbed the bike then and made a dash past him, but he yanked my sleeve and pulled me back.

"You tryin' to run out on me, boy? I risk all to get you across that river. You think I just do it for good times?" He reached up and snatched at my coat front, banty that he was.

I shoved him away. He stumbled backward, but didn't go down. "That's all I have, mister. I do thank you for the crossing. That knife is the best of its kind." In a burst I pushed smartly up the road.

"You win," he grunted, then hollered, "I'll settle for a bottle. I know you got a bottle in them bags, boy."

"I got no bottle, mister," I yelled, pushing fast around the first switchback.

My shoes squished with every step, and I shivered as a breeze struck my soaked trousers. Now at the top of the grade faint moonlight showed the road's direction and gave shadows to rocks and ruts. But I was tired to the point of helplessness; soon I would have to find a proper place to bed down. Around a bend a scatter of buildings with logs and scrap lying about looked to be an abandoned mill. No blaze in the burner; no lights in the big house behind the rough cabins along the road.

In front of the first cabin I laid down the wheel and stepped onto the small porch. "Hello in there?" From the house around back, a lamp flickered to life, as several dogs sounded their alarm. At this hour I'd best announce I was up to no mischief. The dogs, only two but barking like ten, bounded around the side of the cabin to stand foursquare, blocking my way. The light inside the house moved past a window and stopped. I let the dogs sniff my hand, as I talked to them. They still barked, but looked willing to allow me by, so I summoned a brisk walk to the log house's front stoop. The lamp now shone from somewhere behind the door.

"I mean no harm," I hollered. "Traveling by bicycle. Need a place to sleep. Could I please use the floor in one of the cabins?"

The dogs never stopped. The lamp light shifted. After several long moments, a woman's voice called, "Cabin in front. Floor's clean."

"Thank you very much, ma'am." I hauled the wheel inside the little shack. The door didn't quite close, but enough to keep the dogs out. In the stone-cold dark of the windowless room I felt for a wall and leaned the bike against it, wettest bag to the outside. The blanket I spread on the floor to dry. My stomach tight with hunger, I curled up next to another wall and meant to take my shoes off, but my eyes had already fastened shut.

32

❀   ❀   ❀

I found I had lost the hose to the pump and the front tire was
soft so I walked on to Toledo.

FROM A LETTER TO THE *SANTA ROSA PRESS DEMOCRAT*

Yawning powerfully, I stood in the cabin doorway stretching
myself awake. The sun hung well above the trees; no early
start this day. Come noon Ray would be at the Chehalis Post
Office. Now I'd be pressed to get there by early afternoon, and then
only if I found good roads.

The bags and spread-out blanket had dried little. On opening the
bags though, I blessed Ray's mother for the quality of canvas she
used to make them; few items were damp, and those would soon
dry on the handlebars. Digging around for dry socks, two pair, I put
them both on to fend the wet of the shoes. My block-S jersey was
dry, and I snaked into it. The blanket I folded and hung over the
top tube, then wheeled outside. Once underway, I'd unfold it, let it
flap from the back of the bike. The cyclometer was at eight hundred
ninety-five miles, forty-six I'd racked up yesterday. Still, the late
travel had cost me part of the morning.

Obliged to give my thanks to the woman of the house, I pushed
around the corner of the cabin, past a clump of white daisies, and
lifted and dropped the front wheel. For sure the tire was soft. I'd
give it a good pump after I'd made my manners. Crossing the long
grass between the cabin and the log house was enough to alert the
dogs. The commotion brought the woman to the front door where
she stood surveying me. "Quiet down, Belle, Clem." To me, "Your
jersey says you're a school boy. You hungry, son?"

"Well, yes, ma'am, sure. I came to give my thanks for the cabin
floor last night. I'm through school. Just hang on to the jersey for
old times."

She laughed a from-low-down laugh. More than middle age and
of ample size, she had an open face and kind eyes. "Park your

bicycle in the sun so that blanket can dry and come 'round back. I'll scare up something to eat."

"You're mighty kind, ma'am."

"Glad for the company," she said, when I met her at the back door. "You fooling around the river how you got wet? Sit over there." She waved a hand at the big round table and a chair nearest the pantry. "Won't take me a minute to dish up." Heavy all around, the woman was light on her feet, and moved with easy grace over the green linoleum to the big Acme range.

"Got wet on the crossing, ma'am." I sat where she said. "I'm much in debt for the night's rest. I'll be pleased to do chores after." Ray would understand even if it meant a longer wait for him.

The large kitchen smelled of bacon and fresh-baked bread, starting my saliva good. Reaching over the several kettles on the back holes, the woman lifted the broad door of the range's high closet and took out one, and another, and a third covered pan while I told her about our trip, the paper, Ray. She set before me a plate heaped with bacon and ham too, three fried eggs and a mound of fried potatoes.

"This looks like about the best meal I ever saw."

Across the table she sat smiling at me, both hands around a large white cup of coffee. I smiled back, my mouth full, and tried to eat some slower, but food never tasted so good.

"Say you came across the river, but the ferry's last run is midnight. It was close on 1:30 when Clem and Belle got riled. I had the shotgun trained on the door. You were to make a rattle of that knob I'd have blasted you, boy, asked who you were later." She took my empty plate. "More eggs and potatoes?"

"Can't say no, ma'am, good as they are. I'm most sorry to put a fright in you last night. The ferryman came for me in his rowboat when I hollered to him. His barge ran aground on the midnight crossing."

"Again? Tobias is forever grounding that tub, and no cause but his own. Truth now, was he sober enough to row that toy boat he built?" She laughed her deep laugh and set my plate down with helpings near as large as the first. "Must have given you a wet ride. Boat's too small for one passenger. And you with a bicycle and all."

"I was grateful. He made a special trip for me."

"Miserable little man. Us in these parts been trying to get another ferryman on this crossing. He charge you?"

"I didn't have money for fare, so I gave him my knife. I think it was enough."

"He took your knife? It's a free crossing. No fare required. He's paid a good wage. No cause to bilk folks." Her round face scowled then softened. "Can I get you some more?"

"Thank you, ma'am, but I'm full to the top. Now I'd like to chop you some wood, or do whatever else." She stood up and I did too, patting my stomach so she'd know I liked her cooking.

"One side the barn there's wood. Ax and hatchet are in the stump. Be a help if you'd split some, fill the box. Coal scuttle here is for kindling, if you have time."

"My friend wouldn't have me not do chores for a night's lodging and a generous meal, ma'am." I crossed the yard with Belle and Clem happy at my heels, my thoughts tangled. A free crossing and that Tobias fellow not only took my knife but was ready to fight me for the billiken too.

The wood was already cut to lengths, dry, with no knots. Easy, fast splitting. A chunk on its end, ax swung high, strike so solid it telegraphed to my bones, the two pieces falling one side and the other. In a queer sort of way, chopping wood made a man feel altogether a man. When I'd filled the box, I carried the rest of the pieces in to the barn and added them to the neat stack along the wall. Kindling took more attention, but the hatchet brought me closer to the sweet smell of fir, and the scuttle was stuffed in no time.

The good woman thanked me and handed me a package in brown grocery paper. "Sandwiches enough for Ray too." Big smile. "Now get yourself on down that road."

"Thanks, ma'am. I doubt there'll be any left for old Ray."

Once out of sight of the house, I stopped to spread the blanket over the back, drape the damp shirt and socks over the handlebars, and give the front tire some needed air. Unstrapping the pump, it took a moment to recognize what I saw: no hose. Probably lost it hefting the bike in and out of that boat. Now it would be push and plod the several miles on to Toledo, where I'd hope for a bike shop. If Ray had money left, I'd buy a hose in Chehalis.

Grateful for the level road, I walked fast, covering ground, miles, until one last right angle turn and I was in the little town of Toledo. A left at the drug store brought me to Main Street and a bicycle shop. The fellow let me use his air pump, while he fired questions at me about how had I made the trip all the way from California. I told him that what passed for roads weren't always what we could ride on. I pointed to the cyclometer. "My friend and I walked maybe half those miles." His eyes widened, and I was pleased I'd asked to use his pump.

The other side of the bridge north of town the road was nothing but winding, steep grade and more push until, at the top it leveled off, and I hopped on. But around the bend the surface turned to old corduroy, its ancient logs in deep decay impossible to ride on. Trees to either side thinned now: a few firs, marshy undergrowth, willows, cottonwood with most of the leaves already down. Overhead, clouds had gathered in leaden piles. I missed Ray's watch, but the direction of the sun would say past noon. I pictured him standing outside the Post Office. He'd pull out his watch, peer down the street. No Victor. No, Vic was afoot, barely north of Toledo, his stomach round with food, while his best friend waited.

A raindrop plopped on the bill of my cap. Another.

Drops grew heavier, harder. I yanked the blanket, almost dry, off the back, and grabbed the shirt and socks from the handlebars to stuff them down the bags. Abruptly, the old corduroy quit. I mounted to ride between the ruts of the almost straight, nearly level road through what looked to be prairie country. Here I might make up some time, maybe pull in to Chehalis by middle afternoon.

Rain let up some to return even heavier, now driven by a stiff breeze, but the wind at my back sent me along at good clip. It was past mid-afternoon when I reached the little town of Forest. The rain had eased, but the clouds still kept the sun to themselves. At the town pump I filled my canteen and washed mud from my hands and bags, while an old man watering his horse told me the road to Chehalis was passable good and only some more than seven miles.

Out of town, after crossing a long trestle bridge that spanned a vast slough, I puzzled about the forks in the road with no sign boards. I stayed with the planks. After a couple of miles this proved the wise course, a board on a tree plainly saying Chehalis. Countryside was wooded now, cedar and fir. Rain turned heavy. Well into afternoon and the sun gone from the world, the wind at my back brought chill.

Fretting about whether Ray's sores might be so bad he wouldn't be able to ride the hundred miles on to Seattle, I pumped hard to a crest. There, half a mile or so ahead, lay the buildings of what had to be Chehalis, and my load was lighter. Planking took me not only to town, but most of the way onto Market Street. Around the corner of Cascade Avenue a Post Office flag swung in lazy furls above a handsome building. Dismounting in front of it, I looked about, at the front steps, down the street, up, across. No Ray, anywhere.

33

⊛ ⊛ ⊛

I had not made the trip as quick as we figured. Ray thought something had happened to me. We were glad to be together again, and started at once for the ranch owned by his uncle. We have been waiting here until the wheel could be repaired and the rains cease.

FROM THEIR LETTER TO THE *SANTA ROSA PRESS DEMOCRAT*

The clerk in the Post Office said a young fellow had waited around for his buddy until a while ago, but didn't say where he was going when he left. Outside at the bike I worried through my choices, as I watched a team of two, still harnessed together, running down Market Street, folks in a wild scatter hollering "runaways." I could come back tomorrow at noon, when Ray would likely return; or I could stay put awhile, see if he showed up. But what if he'd had trouble with some stumble-stone, couldn't get here at all?

"You made it!" Ray sprinted around the corner of the Post Office. We grabbed each other as if we'd been apart a month.

"I was around back talking to a fellow just in from Forest." Ray's words spilled like pebbles from a bucket, and he kept clapping me on the back. "Said he saw no wheeler along the way. So I judged you met trouble south of Forest. All the time old Victor was out there ahead of him." He jabbed my arm with his elbow and couldn't stop smiling. I chuckled in spite of myself. "Got some sandwiches here, made by a woman gave me a place to sleep last night."

He shot me a look, like how could I so quickly fall to sin. Savoring his torment, I took a long moment before telling of the cabin and the woman feeding me breakfast. We sat there on the steps eating, while the mist turned to light rain. I told him of the ferryman taking the jackknife for fare, then the woman saying the crossing was free. I left out about the billiken and my travel frights the night before.

He sneezed and coughed.

"Got the grippe?"

"Must have caught it last night. Slept in a drafty loft."

"At your uncle's?"

"No. Yesterday I picked up a letter from Mama. Said Uncle Lloyd lives about five miles out of town, so I decided to wait for you."

"Where was this loft?"

"Livery stable down Market." He chomped into another sandwich and sneezed again.

"Let's get in out of the wet." I picked up the wrappings and the last two sandwiches. Inside, we hunkered down by the writing table. "How are the sores?" I asked under my breath.

"Still ugly." Sitting on his haunches, he leaned against a leg of the table. A proper-looking lady, in a flow of rain cape and looking like the pictures of Queen Wilhelmina swept through the door.

"So what about your bike?"

"Brazier sent to Centralia for new head and top tubes. Said the metal was too fatigued to hold that braze in Grants Pass. Pieces'll come by stage Saturday, tomorrow, but he can't fix the bike till Monday. Going to cost three dollars and fifty cents, Vic. My train ticket was two dollars."

"Good we had the money. Leaves us two dollars seventy cents? And I lost the hose to my pump on that fool boat ride. After a hose, maybe leaves us two dollars. That get us up there, you think?" The Queen lady glanced down at me, and her cape brushed my trouser as she swirled past.

"Won't cost us anything tomorrow and Sunday at Uncle Lloyd's and Aunt Josie's."

"But Monday is September 27. It's near a hundred miles yet. October 1 is when Finley said to get the money and fair passes from the *Post Intelligencer*."

"We can do it." Ray coughed.

"And you feeling poorly, topside and backside both."

"Now don't get in a twitch. I'll feel good by Monday."

The lady was deep into reading a letter as she aimed for the door. Worried she might bang into it, I jumped up and opened it for her. "Thank you, young man," she said, but her eyes didn't smile, just returned to the letter before she was through the door.

Ray deposited our last paper wrap in the rubbish bin and followed me out. Rain had stopped. Late sun slanted through tumbles of puffy white clouds in a very blue sky.

"Your mother tell how to find your uncle's?"

"North of town about half a mile and turn left. Follow that near four miles." He took my bike and pushed out onto Cascade Street.

By the Veeder it was some better than four miles when we saw what had to be Ray's uncle's farm at the end of a lane through a field of corn stalks. Tall poplars bordered a house and barn. As we pulled up at the pump house around back, Uncle Lloyd came out to meet us. Balding, heavy-bearded and barrel-chested, he had a gladness in his eye and a strong handshake. "Good to see you boys. On your way to the Exposition, Sis says. Just one wheel? Leave it against the wall there." He motioned us to follow him up the back steps.

"My wheel is getting put back together in town, Uncle Lloyd. Won't be fixed till Monday. We'd like to stay until then, if it's all right with you and Aunt Josie."

"Son, your busted bike is our happy providence."

Aunt Josie, wiping her hands on her apron, met us at the door to the big, screened porch. "Come on in. I just set supper out." She was a bony woman almost as tall as Uncle Lloyd, and led us in to the kitchen and the big, round table covered over with a white oilcloth.

We told them about our trip, and Santa Rosa, and our families. Aunt Josie said the cots on the sleeping porch were all made up for us. She knew just what to do for Ray's grippe, and saddle sores were same as bedsores; she had a trusty remedy. Uncle Lloyd said before daybreak we'd go with him to cut wood.

After Ray and I had polished off her fine roast beef supper and downed two helpings apiece of berry cobbler, Aunt Josie showed us out to the cots. We'd barely flopped and she was through the door again with a mug of barley water and a mustard plaster for Ray. "Tomorrow when you boys get back from work, I'll have you some wheat gruel. And more barley water, Ray. Now, Victor, don't you come near Ray when he coughs."

We'd no sooner settled than she was back, this time her arms full of bottles, bowls, cloths and a basin of steaming water. "Over you go," she ordered Ray. "We're going to fix those nasties on your rusty-dusty." Poor fellow turned himself over, his speckled backside gleaming like a rubbed hog in the light of the lamp she set by the cot. He yipped when she first went at him, cleaning his sad bottom with hot water and bar soap, but then barely muttered every now and then. Here he just met his Aunt Josie, now he lay there showing her the very place God split him.

"A little vinegar coming, son. Won't hurt much." She doused a cloth and cleaned his hide again. Ray's mumbles came louder, but never amounted to complaint. With a soft towel she dried him off so gently, taking such care with those fiery boils. Next, she daubed a square of chamois in a bowl of white powder. "Potato flour." She dusted his bottom. "Starch starves those miseries. They just curl up and die." She laughed a girl's laugh. I liked her. Ray did too, I could tell, in spite of the abuse she'd heaped on him.

Next morning, the sun still well behind the Cascades, Ray and I scrambled up into the wagon among the axes and saws. Uncle Lloyd climbed onto the seat and headed the horses down a rough trail. We rattled and jounced maybe three quarters of a mile before coming to an island of uncleared, gently rolling ground. The Pliny woods, Uncle Lloyd called it, not saying why.

Once we'd tied the animals with enough rein they could get at the grass, we each of us picked a tree to light our axes into. Ray and I swung hard as Uncle Lloyd, but his strikes were to better effect. His good-sized alder soon came thudding down, while Ray and I still chopped away at his maple and my oak. Ray's tree creaked and swayed before it fell, just as my oak toppled. Uncle Lloyd limbed his tree in a steady rhythm. "Your mother tells us you aim to be a minister, Ray."

Ray's feet sought safe purchase in the thicket of his tree's lower branches. "Yes, sir, our Lord permitting."

"Ministry is a fine calling. And you, young Victor, your plans take you beyond that fair?"

"I'd like to go to college, sir." I stood on my felled log, palms resting on the end of my ax handle. "My Uncle Ben offered me the money. But I'd take no pride in the borrowing."

"Take your uncle's money, son. Then pay him back. With interest."

"I'd like to, sir. But I don't know."

Uncle Lloyd talked as fast as he chopped. "Now that University of Washington up in Seattle, there's a school will have some mighty handsome buildings after the fair. Twelve big exhibition halls on their property." He left off chopping to draw deeply on his cigarette. "My, wouldn't I like to grab a bicycle and tag along with you young bucks."

Ray pulled himself straight, sweating, pale. Uncle Lloyd stubbed his smoke on the log, took up his saw and more talk. "Josie, she'd sooner be off to that Washington in the District of Columbia, see the suffragettes' new headquarters. She's all for getting women the vote. Makes me proud of her."

Around noon Aunt Josie showed up with a hamper of lunch, having carried it all the way from the house. We sat on the logs and ate in the soft rain.

It was near 4:00 by Ray's watch, and him mighty tuckered, when we had the wagon heaped with wood. Three big piles were left for Uncle Lloyd to haul another day. I heisted myself up on top of the load, then gave Ray a hand. His trembled. After dinner that night, and Sunday night too, Ray endured Aunt Josie's remedies on his chest and bottom. His cough seemed no better, though on Sunday he said he felt stronger and his sores showed healing.

Sunday afternoon Uncle Lloyd and I looked about in his barn until he found a hose to fit my pump. I set to attaching it almost before I'd finished my thanks. Aunt Josie said she was willing to break the sabbath by baking cookies, and Ray told her he thought the Lord wouldn't mind. By Monday noon, when we figured Ray's wheel should be mended, Aunt Josie and Uncle Lloyd walked us out to the road. Ray and I clutched our packages of sandwiches and cookies. Aunt Josie told him he should stop often to rest, and he must dust his backside with the potato powder she'd put in his package.

"I'll think of you boys when I pick up those hauls in Pliny woods." Uncle Lloyd grabbed us by the shoulders. "Fine old Roman, Pliny. Loved his woods too." Over his beard, Uncle Lloyd's eyes brimmed. We all bear-hugged. Aunt Josie's cheeks were slick with tears.

Ray and I walked off down the road, and my own tears welled up. We turned every little while to wave to them still standing there at the end of the drive. Around the bend then we left behind the only family we had within almost a thousand miles.

34

❀ ❀ ❀

We are within about ninety miles of Seattle and expect to be
there in a few days. It has rained considerable for the last
three days. . . . We had another breakdown, which delayed
us.

FROM THEIR LETTER TO THE *SANTA ROSA PRESS DEMOCRAT*

We said little on the plod back to Chehalis. Feeling sad
myself, I understood Ray's need for quiet. But at the jog in
the road just before town, he quavered, "Got to throw
up," then stumbled and nearly fell on his way to the ditch. I stayed
on the verge and watched him retch and heave into the blackberry
vines. Afterward he sat clutching his knees, forehead on his folded
arms.

"You gonna make it, chum?" I stood over him.

"I'll sit awhile. May have another go," he said into his knees.

Ray for sure sick, and us nearly a hundred miles from Seattle; it
made a man consider. After a bit, I said, "Think we should head on
back to Uncle Lloyd's? Forget the sappy twenty-five dollars? After
you're well, we could still get up to the fair before it closes."

He raised his head. "Don't worry, Vic. I'm better now."

We took it slow on the walk to the brazier's, only one rest stop
when Ray felt too green, but he didn't lose any more innards. The
brazier was a broad chunk of a fellow, his overalls bulging nobly at
the equator. He was sorry, but a man had come in earlier with his
team's farm collars, the iron overtop on both hames broken. "Has
to get his crop in," he told us. "Bicycle comes second to a man in
true need, you understand."

We just nodded when he said it would be three o'clock before
Ray's bicycle was joined, and ambled off. Ray pulled out his watch.
"Two o'clock. We'll find a bench. Gives me time to get my legs
back."

Promptly at three, our money in hand and Ray's color improved,
we waited while the brazier added air to the tires and showed us the

clean joinings of his brazes. By three-thirty we were pedaling past Uncle Lloyd's road off to the left. I hollered to Ray up there setting our pace, "How about we camp near Centralia? Have a long night's rest?"

"I'm all right, Vic. We can do more than Centralia."

Ray's new tubes gleamed in the afternoon sun, it now making more of a show than it had all day, the clouds having retreated to clumps over the mountains. Planking quit as we passed the fair grounds, but the gravel proved packed enough we stayed mounted to Centralia.

Side by side up Tower Street, we passed saloons with signs welcoming coal miners and shingle stiffs. I glanced over at Ray so we could joke about not being welcome in their saloons. Gaunt and slumped, his whole self labored just to keep his seat, and I swallowed my talk.

After a bridge over what a sign said was the Skookum Chuck River, we stopped to eat one of Aunt Josie's sandwiches and some cookies. Now we laughed together about the river's name and filled our canteens. Ray managed the climb back up the bank, even saying he felt better than he had all day and, "Let's try for Grand Mound or maybe Tenino."

"You lead, so I'll know if you tumble." He threw me a look more like his old self; we could make Seattle in time after all.

The road belonged to us now. Well into supper hour, farm folks' travel was done for the day. But with the low sun still in the sky and the country open, we should have light awhile. Ray even stood to pedal on the hard surface. When we'd crossed the tracks outside Grand Mound, he said he felt like pressing on through Tenino. I knew he was played out; I also knew we had to clock as many miles as he could safely do. Out of Tenino we dismounted for the first real hill, as a freight chuffed up the slight grade on the tracks below. The fireman waved out the cab. I waved back. Ray, ahead, just hunched over the bike. Camp had to be soon.

On the covered bridge across the Deschutes, I said, "We'll bed down here on the river bank. You're too gone for the climb out of this ravine." He was white around the eyes. "Let's make that Olympia road. I can do it."

"But tomorrow's as good."

All this day we hadn't mentioned Olympia, our travel being that much in doubt. At Uncle Lloyd's, studying our map, we had determined the leg of road over to the town of Olympia was almost the same miles as to bypass it on the main road. Santa Rosa folks would like to hear about Washington's state capitol. Also, from Olympia it appeared we might catch our first sight of Peter Puget's Sound, the same water shared with Seattle. It was decided: we would go the Olympia road and have a look.

State Capitol, Olympia, Wash.

But now Ray was emptied. Yet, if we met our plan, it just might put coal back in his burner. So, after a short rest, we pushed on up the hill. The next couple of miles brought one grade after another, until finally, a board pointed to a road off to the left: Olympia.

We made camp right there by the sign. With dark fast settling in the thick woods all about, we chained the bikes not only together but to a tree, then gathered enough wood to keep a fire going all night. Ray's voice came thin and croaky, and I wondered if laryngitis might be claiming it. He blew his nose into the brush a lot, but he coughed only twice, a dry hack.

"How are those cankers on your stern?" I asked, as he unrolled his blanket and I stoked the fire.

"Nearly healed. Aunt Josie saw more of me than she should, but what she saw she sure fixed."

"Barley water and wheat gruel didn't scare off that grippe though."

"Grippe could take longer," he said against the blanket he'd already crawled into, and he scooted nearer the fire.

Getting up was a relief after a cold night and too many animal noises for much sleep. As we tied on the blankets shortly after sun-up, a team of twelve yoked oxen lumbered by, pulling what must have been a log fully fourteen feet across. We nodded and said, " 'Morning," to the two teamsters walking to either side of the animals and carrying long sticks. If the oxen slowed or stopped, the men hollered, "Ho!" and gave the animals a thwack. "Douglas fir,"

Ray said, when they'd bulked on through and we stood blinking at the size of the tree. "Think Santa Rosa would believe us if we told them?"

"I know they wouldn't." I said, glad for his talk and his voice to talk with. "Nearly thirty miles yesterday." I pushed out onto the Olympia road. "Pretty good for a late start and a sick pup."

"We'll make that fair." Ray sounded almost like my old friend again.

The road was graveled, though not lately rolled. We stayed mounted, even on the hills. Ray ahead set the pace. At a summit he stopped astride his bike and gazed north. Pulling up, I saw why. Before us the grand Puget Sound spread great fingers of water with islands and peninsulas clothed in timber scattered between. In the west, jagged, snowy peaks marched in a great phalanx. North across the longest reach of water rose a superb, white peak veiled in distance.

I said softly, "All that wonder gives me the feel of church." Ray tossed me his look, the one that smiled. "Just how would you know?" But he put a hand on my shoulder.

Half way down the grade he braked, stopped, and staggered off the road. As I came up, he was spewing the biscuits he'd had earlier. After he'd gone another round, he sat beside me in the grass. "Only two days left, Vic." He lay back in the grass with his eyes closed. I worried and walked around and drank water for maybe a half hour before Ray eased himself up and said he felt like travel.

Two miles more brought us to Olympia, a pretty town made prettier bordered as it was by the waters. We rode past the fire department as the men washed off a hose wagon and three hose carts. Passing the *Chronicle Republican* office we wondered if they might want to write us up in their paper, but decided we didn't have time to be interviewed. In front of the Capitol Building we stood astraddle the bikes and marveled at the impressive masonry arching the entrance and all the windows. Small six-sided turrets at the corners and entrance matched one giant turret with a fine, six-sided clock. Each clock face showed the proper time: 11:09.

"Let's take a swing down to the water," I suggested, "watch the boats."

"Better we get on up the line, hoss."

I gave him a look to see if he needed to throw up, but he just seemed tired. I dug in my sack for apples and the white cheese Aunt Josie stuffed in. He took a piece of the cheese, drank some water, and we set off.

The road out of town was a steep, mile-long climb on foot and pushing. But the sun warmed and lit up—through stands of fir—a massive white mountain that consumed the eastern sky. "Mt. Rainier," Ray announced. "Around here they likely still call it Mt. Tacoma." He was puffing hard, but stayed the pace.

We stopped often, saying it was to look around at the water, mountains. Once we'd made the climb, we mounted and kept our seats on a finely-rolled surface. What's more, the road ahead looked to be easy swells with no long grades. I fell back. As Ray drew ahead, I recognized his forward hunch, the way he had of trying to save what was left of himself.

At Yelm we rejoined the main road, as a three-seated wagon and a Ford automobile passed us. After the bridge across the Nisqually River we met two farm wagons and a buggy with a fancy top. As each approached, I watched Ray. His course held true. If he was shy on strength, this buddy of mine made up for it in grit. Nearly five miles past Roy Station, sailing along with Ray's track straight as a ruler, we might just hold out for camp in Tacoma. But then, as I watched, his bicycle swerved, weaved side to side, straightened. A few revolutions and it listed left, him slopping with it. And then right, before it and he hung sideways a long moment, then went down.

Ray tumbled off and just lay there, so still.

35

✷ ✷ ✷

We traveled a few miles more and camped near the small town of Dupont, where one of the many Dupont powder works is located.

FROM THEIR LETTER TO THE *SANTA ROSA PRESS DEMOCRAT*

Ray still had his senses but was too weak to get up. Hauling him to his feet, I held him till he steadied. "Sorry," he said, eyes swimming into focus. He was pale but hot to the touch. By holding him so he could walk, we struggled ourselves and the wheels across the main road onto a small road heading left. An arrow pointed toward the water and some place called Dupont. Ray walked on his own now. "Just weak is all, Vic. I'd like to sleep soon as we find a place."

"You're burning up. Sleep is good for a fever."

About a quarter mile down the wooded road, we liked the look of a giant fir with limbs enough to shelter if it rained. He sat down, and I brought him some hard bread and cheese with his canteen. He ate nothing but drank his canteen dry. I unrolled his blanket and put my canteen beside it. Soon as he was down he was asleep, his blanket splotched with afternoon sun filtered through the tree branches.

I chained his bike near and picked up his empty canteen. Ray was safe enough, I could explore whatever was Dupont. Road dirt being hard-packed, I mounted, then gave another look over my shoulder. He hadn't moved, and likely wouldn't for awhile. Riding between forests of cedar and fir, my head was aboil. Ray had turned sicker. Travel, even tomorrow, could be impossible. This was Tuesday. We promised to be at the fair on Friday, October 1st. From where Ray slept, it might be forty, maybe fifty, maybe more miles. If he was still sick tomorrow, could he do fifty miles on Thursday? I would not go to the fair without Ray. A dollar and four bits would buy a telegram to the *Seattle Post Intelligencer* telling them we would be late by how much I didn't know.

Ahead now were buildings, a cart, wagons, several people: Dupont. I rode slowly down the main street. To either side clean houses appeared brand new, a church and school fresh-built. Set among tall firs with a fine stream running through, the town had the look of a well-kept park. Storefront windows of a building on the stream bank displayed an array of merchandise, and I set course.

"I'm Clem Fisher," the man said from behind the counter. "You traveling?"

"Yes, Mr. Fisher. Name is Victor McDaniel. My pal and I are on wheels to Seattle. He's resting just up the road. We biked from California."

Unimpressed, Mr. Fisher said. "To take in that fair, I expect. Well, you won't find anything up there as pretty as Dupont, young man." A back door opened, and I heard the soft burble of the creek.

"Dupont makes some kind of chemicals, doesn't it?"

"Nitroglycerine, lad. Mighty unstable stuff. Started production only a week ago.

"Anything ever explode?" I had to ask. Mr. Fisher and the man warming himself by the stove in the center of the store laughed. "Sure," said Mr. Fisher. "DuPont had his reasons for putting the plant on this much land."

"Sounds like dangerous work," I said, deciding Ray and I would find another camp for tomorrow night if I had to tie him on his bike. Then I remembered. "Could you please direct me to some water, sir? I'd like to fill my buddy's canteen."

"Spring house is around the side, son. Help yourself."

My hand was on the knob when I spied a glass case to one side. In it were several billikens identical to ours. "Are these from the fair?"

"Two-bits each. Patron Spirit of the Alaska-Yukon-Pacific Exposition, God of Things That Ought to Be, they call them. Maybe your pal would like one?"

"I can't buy one, sir. But I do see how one of these little fellows could be a good luck piece for folks to carry around."

The man at the stove said, "You'll go through Tacoma. Be worth your time to take a gander at their new high school. Finest west of Chicago."

"Thanks. And thanks for the water, Mr. Fisher."

In the side yard the roofed-over spring house had a lift-up door with a bucket and dipper alongside. After filling the canteen and drinking long, I was on my way. For supper I would find Dupont's Sequalitchew Creek and catch us a fish or two. Ray was still asleep when I returned, so after chaining my bike to his, I took the pole and lit out.

Later, when I'd built the fire and both fish were sizzling, he stretched and yawned. I said, "Better?" "Better." He did sound stronger. As he sat up, I wasn't sure about the stronger, but he moved more like his body was his friend. He ate the fish and some cheese and bread, and said he'd like to walk down the road, see how his legs worked.

But next morning, Wednesday, he didn't come awake. I waited until I'd had something to eat and gone to the creek to wash up, then I knelt by him and shook his shoulder. "Ray? Ray." His eyes stayed closed. Suddenly frantic, I lifted his arm and felt for pulse. Beat after beat, steady.

"Vic?" he drawled.

"Who'd you expect? Feel like getting up, chum?"

"Still sleepy. I'll stay here awhile."

I wrote another letter, then just sat, bedazed by that king of the sky, Mt. Rainier, or Mt. Tacoma. Whatever folks wanted to call it, it looked like it owned the whole planet. This morning the peak wore an inverted crown of cloud, and wisps of fog arranged themselves in the lower folds of the king's robe.

It was two o'clock in the afternoon before Ray came alert, saying it was high time we put wheel to road, and almost looked like he meant it.

"We know how to get along without that twenty-five dollars, Ray. Our two dollars and seventy cents will buy us all we want to see of that fair when we do get there, maybe next week after you're whole again." If he heard, he paid no mind. Tying his blanket to the bike, he declared, "I'm better than new."

"Then take a look at this, Mr. Better-than-new." I showed him the cyclometer's nine nine nine. "I'll holler up when she turns a thousand." I felt more optimistic by the minute.

We were crossing the tracks at Hillhurst when I hooted at him, and he came back to look. "Say, now," we both let out slow. Finally tearing my eyes from the Veeder's one zero zero zero, I said, "Guess you've earned the right to look a little tattered, old bean." Weakly, he jabbed my shoulder. "Some of the Beau Brummell's gone from you too, pal."

The mileage put some of the giddy in us, but the rest was because we were back on the road. Ray even sat looser in the saddle, his backside healed, his hunch gone, fever spent. Still, late in the afternoon, in the city of Tacoma, about sixteen miles from Dupont,

I yelled over to him, "Tacoma brags they just built the finest high school west of Chicago. If it's all that fine, I'd like to bed down where we can wake up and see it in the morning."

"Good idea."

Soon, standing before the great stone building, we agreed it was a high school to brag about all right. With its backdrop of Puget Sound waters, the massive school looked more like a railroad hotel. Santa Rosa would hear about this.

"Building or no building, I bet you could beat their track team, Vic." I liked that he thought I was a good track man. And he might be right that I could beat these fellows, most of 'em anyway.

In a vacant lot across the street we put our blankets down under a big maple. Soon as we'd eaten, Ray said, "Think I'll roll in." And he was asleep before his prayers. Again I worried.

At first light Thursday I was up and walking slowly all the way around the big high school, before students might arrive. I let my head hear the thoughts it had carried for weeks, about our joyous arrival in the city of Seattle: Two handsome fellows ride grandly in to town, all sweat and smiles and heroic humility. Around them jubilation erupts, as the happy victors are greeted by throngs of cheering people, most of them lovely young women. Now, Ray still asleep on the morning before our scheduled arrival, he could wake up too sick to travel the last thirty miles. I shivered only partly from the cool. Stopping to give the school one last look, I stumbled a sort of silent prayer to Ray's God, telling Him I hoped He'd see to it we got up there to that fair.

Ray was chewing on a piece of hard tack and rolling his blanket when I got back. I said, "You ready to ride?"

"Ready to ride." He sounded almost too hearty.

We headed for town, down Pacific Avenue, past their grand, domed Railroad Station. The day was cloudless. Once on the main road the surface was first class and with no long grades. But Ray got winded, and he still had the paleness. We stopped often, at Pacific City, Auburn, Kent, Orillia, Renton. At each long rest we ate some and drank water. He lay flat on the grass if there was any, then after a half hour or so eased himself to sit, insisting he felt like travel. Each time I knew he was at the bottom of his bag, the rings around his eyes darker at each stop. When he mounted, his hunch was back, along with my frets about how long could he safely ride.

At Georgetown, barely south of Seattle, we pulled off into a ditch. "We'll bed down here," I announced. "Tomorrow's travel will be short. You got to sleep before you tumble off that bike again."

"Dark is fast coming, Vic. I can make Seattle. Be good to see the city when we wake up."

I knew I shouldn't listen to him. But how could I not? I had never wanted anything so much as I wanted to wake up in the morning and see Seattle. "You going to be able to hang on, chum?" He climbed on and shoved out.

I kept a close eye on him ahead of me. For sure no boy or man ever had more git and gumption than my buddy, Ray. Wagons, buggies, automobiles passed us in a steady parade as we neared the city. Night was on us now. A few automobiles and some buggies had lighted their lamps. We should light ours. But one more stop would postpone camp by that much, which was too much. I could hope the vehicles coming at us and passing could see us better than we could see them. I picked up pace to follow closer behind Ray and wondered if folks in the buggy clattering by could have any notion of how far we had come. Or any knowing how much fifty-four days' hard travel cost a couple of wheelers.

A street lamp ahead cast Ray in slumped silhouette. At that instant a thought shuddered through me: What if the *Seattle Post Intelligencer* didn't even remember Finley's arrangement with the *Press Democrat*?

Did I imagine it? Had Ray's bicycle swerved? City or no city, we must find a ditch deep enough to camp and soon. At a slight rise Ray stopped. I pulled alongside. There below and across the water lay a carpet of lights, twice bright reflected in the bay.

"Behind that billboard," he said over the long blare of a boat horn, and pointed to a hill next to the road. Once our blankets were down, a nearly full moon was a yellow melon sliding up from behind the east hills. We stood in front of the big billboard advertising Alt Heidelberg beer and looked out at the city of our dreams. Winking lights beyond the water were a vast firefly quilt, spread over a bed of rolling hills. The farthest hill was most gloriously lighted.

"The A.Y.P.E," Ray almost whispered. We stood there for more time than I know, just looking, feeling what we saw clear to our toetips. Tears backed up behind my eyes and watered down my cheeks. Ray's lips moved in prayer.

Then I noticed, peeking from his pocket, the billiken. He'd stuck him there so the little fellow could see his home town.

Afterword

ON SUNDAY, OCTOBER 3, 1909, THE FOLLOWING ARTICLE APPEARED IN THE *SEATTLE POST INTELLIGENCER*

California Boys End Long Bicycle Ride—Report Some Bad Roads Between Santa Rosa and Oregon—Walk 200 Miles

Two Santa Rosa High School boys arrived in city after a fifty-four day bicycle trip from Santa Rosa, California. Victor McDaniel and Ray Francisco left Santa Rosa on the morning of August 9. They wrote weekly stories of their adventures on the road to a California newspaper. "We went by easy stages on the first few days of the trip,' said McDaniel, 'making a little over thirty miles the first day. After we came accustomed to riding we gradually increased our riding distance daily. We made sixty-four miles one day.

"The roads through the Sacramento Valley kept up by the California Automobile Club were in splendid condition and were the best we encountered on the whole trip.

"On roads in Northern California and Southern Oregon because of the hills we walked about two hundred miles. We cooked our meals and slept out doors when we were unable to find lodging."

The boys will stay two weeks visiting the exposition and will send stories to the Press Democrat of their impressions of the fair. James A. Wood Chief of Exposition yesterday presented the boys with free passes to the exposition during their stay in this city.

Reprinted with permission, Seattle Post-Intelligencer

For more than a week Vic and Ray savored the marvels of Seattle's Alaska-Yukon-Pacific-Exposition. When it closed, the adventurers returned home by train to a fine town welcome arranged by the *Santa Rosa Press Democrat*.

Both served in the Army during World War I, Victor in France, Ray in the United States. After the war, each married and had one daughter.

Vic received a degree in business from the University of Southern California, then worked most of his life for the California Pacific Gas and Electric Company. In retirement he and his wife moved near their daughter on Vashon Island, Washington.

Ray answered his life's calling, becoming a minister to serve churches in California and Washington. He too spent his retirement in Washington, in the town of Lynnwood.

Through the years the men maintained letter contact, but it was only shortly before each died in old age that they met in Lynnwood, Washington, for an afternoon of poignant reminiscence.

Photographs and Postcards

page i: Ray Francisco (right) and Vic McDaniel.

page 9: Postcard of State Hospital for the Insane, Napa, California.

page 14: Postcard of Vacaville, California, from High School Hill.

page 25: Postcard of Mount Lassen, near Red Bluff, California.

page 51: Postcard of bridges on the trail, Shasta Springs, California.

page 62: Postcard of Mount Shasta from Sisson, California.

page 91: Postcard of a 2 hours catch by Jim and Frank Burns in the Rogue River, Oregon.

page 97: Postcard of Sixth Street, Grants Pass, Oregon.

page 98: Postcard of Oregon County Road.

page 109: Postcard of Oakland, Oregon.

page 110: Postcard of Music Mine, Bohemia, near Cottage Grove, Oregon.

page 120: Postcard of campus scene, University of Oregon, Eugene, Oregon.

page 121: Postcard of Villard Hall, State University (now University of Oregon), Eugene, Oregon.

page 125: Postcard of bird's-eye view of the business district, Salem, Oregon.

page 131: Postcard of Chamber of Commerce Building, Portland, Oregon.

page 136: Postcard of ferry crossing the Columbia River by moonlight between Portland, Oregon, and Vancouver, Washington.

page 168: Postcard of University of Washington, Seattle, Washington.

page 171: Postcard of State Capitol, Olympia, Washington.

page 180: Official postcards of auditorium, Alaska-Yukon-Pacific Exposition, Seattle, Washington (top); and of the California Building at the Alaska-Yukon-Pacific Exposition, Seattle, Washington (below), described as "the largest state building at the Exposition. The wide range of productions: mining, wheat growing, lumbering, orange and fruit growing, are all shown in a very masterful and attractive manner."